Sexual Detours

Sexual Detours

Infidelity

and Intimacy

at the Crossroads

Dr. Holly Hein

ST. MARTIN'S GRIFFIN ✦ NEW YORK

www.stmartins.com

Book design by Donna Sinisgalli

Library of Congress Cataloging-in-Publication Data

Hein, Holly.
    Sexual detours: the startling truth behind love, lust, and infidelity /
Holly Hein.
        p.   cm.
    Includes bibliographical references.
    ISBN 0-312-25335-4 (hc)
    ISBN 0-312-27277-4 (pbk)
    1. Adultery—United States—Psychological aspects.   I. Title.
HQ806.H45   2000
306.73'6—dc21   00-023902
                                                           CIP

First St. Martin's Griffin Edition: April 2001

D10 9 8 7 6 5 4 3 2 1

To my precious, challenging,

and ever-affirming children,

Noëlle and Nicolas—

I dedicate this book.

Contents

PART THREE

Finale

Acknowledgments

This could be a very long story because there are so many people I wish to acknowledge. All of these people contributed in no small way to this book.

One sunny August afternoon three years ago, I stood in my friends Ken and Patti's kitchen. We started talking about a book I wanted to write. Several topics piqued my interest. I chose sex. Little did I know that fate was pulling the strings, and that sex with all its illicit excitement and humiliating revelations would even make its way into the hallowed halls of our government in its unexpurgated version.

Many of my patients, both single and married, who were in a relationship or were craving one, had distorted views of sex and marriage. They lived together and slept together, but they knew very little about each other. I wanted to write about the subject of sex and infidelity in order to teach people how to forge stronger, more grounded, and more intimate relationships. I wanted to teach people to understand that in order to make choices that would fulfill their physical, emotional, and spiritual selves, they need to grow whole—whole enough to separate fact from fantasy and love from lust, and to rework all of this into an intimate bond. It is amazing to me that so much is known about sex, but so little is understood on a deep emotional level. Hence, the name of the book: *Sexual Detours*.

I wish to thank Leslie, who is my good friend and right hand. She helped me stay motivated throughout the proposal and first two chapters. Enter David Codikow, who so generously gave me his legal counsel and heartfelt advice. He led me to my wonderful agent, Kim Witherspoon. She took a chance on a nonpublished writer and sold the book to Laura Yorke, whom I consider a person of fine professional substance and stamina who stayed with me throughout the process. They have both become good and valued friends. The publishing business, being what it is, led me to Lara Asher, whose fine editing brought the book you see before you to completion.

I would like to acknowledge many of my other good friends who know what they've done along the way: Ron, who always felt my voice was worth being heard; Caroline, who years ago wanted me to write a book (but as a single mom with two kids to raise, a full practice, and the completion of a doctorate, I couldn't have done it any sooner); Holly and Ava, my soul sisters; John; Ami; Stuart; Afton; Bill; my brother Orrin; Nick M.; Lynette; Irma; Reba; Edna Mae, who took care of those whom I loved; Bill S.; Marshall; Keith; Dan; Michael and Janet; Peter and Nicole; sweet Maryam; dear, dear Tarquin; and Samoan Barish.

In Nature there is sound and silence.
In love it is the same. Listen . . .

Sexual
Detours

PART ONE

Prelude

Chapter One

❦

The Voice of an Affair

> In the middle of the road of life
> I found myself in a dark wood
> Having strayed from the straight path.
>
> —DANTE, *THE DIVINE COMEDY: INFERNO*

❧ *Affair.* The word breathes. It's palpable. It evokes emotions that swamp the senses. For those caught up in the whirlwind, love beckons. Lust and longing rule. Passion is awakened. We are filled with yearning, desire, exhilaration, and freedom. Alive. For others, the word *affair* strikes at gut level. Jealousy and rage. Loss and abandonment. The horror of betrayal vies with the chill of fear. The calamity shakes our soul to the very core.

I believe that *everyone* involved in an affair suffers deeply, for an affair is an assault upon the rock of fidelity. Fidelity is the hearthstone upon which we build our homes and families. Fidelity is where we invest our hopes and dreams. Fidelity is the last bastion for us all. When a partner takes a sexual detour from marriage vows—whether vows were echoed in vaulted cathedrals or whispered in secret—silence falls. A world shatters. And it is to those who live in these shattered worlds that I try to bring a semblance of understanding and growth, helping them heal and grow whole again.

In this book, I want to clarify that at its deepest level, an affair is a betrayal of the self. An affair tells us the story of a shadowed self, a part of ourselves about which we feel uncertain, a self that is not whole or authentic. Self is that combination of feelings, thoughts, and actions unique to each one of us. There are parts of ourselves that we do not allow ourselves to feel or to know, and often the first symptom of this lack of an intimate connection with ourselves is an affair.

An affair, or a sexual detour as I prefer to call it, is an avoidance. A path around a bruised or damaged part of ourselves, not only a sexual detour around the marriage. An affair is an immediate reaction to a present circumstance and lets us avoid dealing with conflict by providing an alternate choice. The underlying issues have roots that reach far into the past. An affair is a cover story, a curtain, a shadow play for a story begun long ago, buried in the unconscious, that is being replayed in the present. This drama takes place offstage, in the wounded, hidden aspects of the self that remain unknown. Because unconscious reasons are out of our awareness, we give ourselves rationales for an affair that often have nothing to do with the real drama within.

All of us who have been in any way touched by an affair seek answers. To my patients, no matter on which side of an affair they find themselves, I repeat the same litany: A sexual detour has little to do with sexual chemistry and a lot to do with the chemistry of escape. It has little to do with the ability to have great sex and a lot to do with the inability to communicate on an intimate level. The truth is that an affair is more about who we are, what we are afraid of, how we handle our conflicts—both within ourselves and in our marriage—than about the third party in the triangle.

In an affair, the betrayed marriage partner usually symbolizes the anxiety or conflict from which we seek to escape, and our fantasies center around the new sexual partner who promises a ticket to freedom. A marriage partner is often the one whom we blame for our problems. The reason for this is simple: Happily, a marriage partner usually means that we have found someone in whom to invest all our hopes and dreams. Unhappily, this means that he or she becomes heir to the impossible task of fulfilling them. No one can accomplish this herculean task. No one can fulfill our unspoken longings and heal all the wounds within. In marriage, if we lay the unfinished task of growing up and growing whole at the feet of our marital partner, he or she may begin to represent what we want to avoid.

The Meaning Behind a Sexual Detour

Our childhood experiences are replayed in our intimate adult relationships. Wounds sustained in childhood shape the wishes we hold for our adulthood and the nature of our adult interaction. When our adult reality does not match those unfulfilled childhood wishes, we *react*. The most common reaction is flight. When we escape from a current conflict by engaging in the flight to a sexual affair, we may believe that new wounds in the present have triggered our behavior. The truth, however, is that past experiences fuel both the nature of the issues and the manner in which we choose to address or to escape those issues. In this way the drama of our early lives is replayed in the present.

Escape from intimacy with a marital partner via the route of a sexual detour allows us to avoid confronting conflicts from these earlier relationships. Shying away from acknowledging or revealing these vulnerable parts of ourselves prevents us from attaining true intimacy, because we express our unresolved conflicts in behavior that harms our relationships and avoids resolution. We seek escape instead of confrontation and insightful solutions.

I tell my patients—especially the ones who do not want to hear it—that, in the deepest sense, a sexual detour has nothing to do with another person. It's about our inability to build intimacy into the marital relationship—indeed, into *any* intimate relationship. It is about who we are and how we feel at the center of our being. It is about what we want. What we fear. What we are afraid to feel. What we cannot allow ourselves to have or to be. It is about what is unknown. Unattended. Unfulfilled. In search of this fulfillment, we sometimes wander alone, lost on a sexual detour.

The desire for more sex is rarely the reason behind the affair, even when sexuality is a major component of the affair. The driving force of sexuality in an affair may simply provide a feel-good escape. Despite the physical intimacy of a sexual affair, sexual detours represent an escape from intimacy. The task of creating marital intimacy requires dealing with frustrations, problems, anxieties. Infidelity, which isolates us from our own pain, offers distance from the problems, not solutions. An affair is about emotional alienation. An affair is not about what we find with somebody else. It's about us. It's about what we cannot find in ourselves.

Intimacy and the Self

Intimacy is something we all want. And why not? Intimacy offers some great benefits. Intimacy with our inner self bestows upon us a sense of confidence and security. When we develop a good sense of ourselves—intimacy with what is within—we are able to express ourselves creatively, bond with others, and risk being genuinely vulnerable. We can have our needs met if only for the simple reason that we know what they are. Intimacy lends hope and infuses us with a sense of well-being.

In order to become intimate with another, we first have to be able to be intimate with ourselves. A sexual detour sends us farther down the road from dealing with the problems within. We may substitute sex, and even marriage, for the self-knowledge necessary for true intimacy. It is only in the discovery of deep personal truths that we emerge as whole, authentic, and capable of achieving true and lasting intimacy.

Intimacy is a catchword for a host of feelings we all want. But at its heart, what does it mean? Intimacy is revealing to ourselves, then to a partner, all our fears, wishes, hopes, and dreams. Who we are inside. Knowing ourselves is one task of adulthood, and communicating that knowledge is the task of forming a relationship. When we each have the freedom and ability to reveal who we are and are accepted, we will be *heard and seen* in the relationship and will have established an intimate connection.

Being heard has nothing to do with hearing, and *being seen* has nothing to do with vision, but they both have everything to do with having emotional needs met. Being heard and seen for who we are gives us the sense of being valued, approved, accepted. Having needs met is a crucial state in infancy when survival is at stake. This translates to emotional survival in adulthood.

Many fears interfere with our ability to be intimate with ourselves or another. Feeling what is inside may simply be too painful or anxiety-provoking for us to face. The fears, anxieties, and wounds covered up by an affair are mainly unconscious ones of which we are unaware. We may be afraid to endure the pain of growth. We may suffer fear of disapproval. Fear that we cannot compete or achieve. Fear of making a choice or taking responsibility. Fear of consequence. Fear of no consequence. With fear couching our every move, we escape to a sexual detour instead and bury there what we cannot handle in reality.

Intimacy with Another

Intimacy with another requires us to be comfortable enough with who we are and have a good enough sense of self-worth to achieve closeness and union without feeling overwhelmed by fear of abandonment or fear of control. The fear of abandonment, and of control, interfere with the development of intimacy. When these fears operate in a relationship, they create distance instead of an intimate exchange. These fears are caused by our very early mothering experiences, which were interpreted at the infantile and childish levels at which they occurred. In the intimate relationships of adulthood, these experiences continue to color our relationships with highly charged emotions.

Building intimacy into a relationship requires learning how to deal with the feelings that provoke a fear of intimacy, instead of running from them. I often tell my patients that their fears of loss and abandonment, or fears of control, no longer represent the same things they experienced as infants and children, even if the feelings remain the same. Feelings aren't facts. As adults we can learn to handle those feelings that interfere with intimacy instead of allowing them to provoke us into flight from intimacy. They don't believe me at first, of course, but sooner or later they do.

A common understanding among therapists is that the lower the quality of marital emotional intimacy, as reflected by our ability to communicate and solve problems, the more likely we are to have an affair. We often make the mistake of believing that the act of being married will provide intimacy and prevent infidelity. Marriage does not carry a guarantee of intimacy, nor does it prevent affairs. Marriage is only a container, an arena wherein intimacy can—if we allow it—occur. Relationships carry risk. Potential. Washing machines carry guarantees.

Intimacy and Sexual Detours

A sexual detour need not be catastrophic, either for ourselves or our marriages. An affair is not a cardinal sin. It is not even a dream come true. But even just a brief fling is something to which we must pay attention, something we must try to understand. A sexual detour presents us with a crisis of opportunity. Sexual detours can motivate us to look into ourselves and finally see who we really are—or want to be. If properly decoded, a sexual detour can lead us toward a path of self-knowledge, growth, and authenticity—toward intimacy. If we understand the hidden meaning, we can empower ourselves and enrich our lives. We must recognize a sexual detour as a sign. A signal. A flag.

It seems easy enough, this business of intimacy, of knowing ourselves. But in truth, understanding ourselves and feeling vulnerable are difficult. We run the other way as fast as we can. Why? Because we're human. We avoid reflection and the intimacy that inner knowledge offers because of the anxiety this process generates. We refrain from introspection because we've been taught an easier route, one that passes for the real thing. We have not been well schooled in the hard work of attaining a whole, integrated self or in the art of forging an intimate connection. Literally and figuratively, we live in an unconscious world. Our culture promotes quick fixes and easy escape. Give me. Get me. Buy me. Illicit dust colors the landscape of love. Sex sells.

The scent of sexual allure, the fragrance of seduction, carries names like Obsession, Jealousy, Joy, Passion. Conversely, survival depends on institutions with names like Fidelity, Trust, Vanguard. We are expected to make our lives cohesive with elements as disparate as oil and water. Lust. Longing. Fantasy. Denial. We are largely taught an ethic that undermines lasting intimacy. We've inherited a paradox.

One of my first cases exemplified this cultural legacy of ours to an extreme degree. Irene and Zachary were as green in the business of relationships as I was in treating them. They were in desperate straits. Irene felt disillusioned, confused, helpless, and hopeless. Her self-esteem drained out of her with every drop of new beauty lotion. Zachary, her husband of two years, was equally beside himself about the marriage and even less intact. The marriage was in a downward spiral. They dangled on the brink of a divorce. Or an affair. Whichever came first. Fortunately, I did.

Since their marriage, Irene had presented herself every evening fully made up and glamorously decked out. If they didn't have sex, she felt rejected and unloved. Zachary, for his part, felt inadequate and anxious. The only reaffirmation of self-worth for either of them depended on her successful seduction. Sexual encounters were tense. All of them were silent. The diamond of their marriage held no facets. Certainly no intimacy. Not a shred of communication. Sexual allure was the key. The crucial element was arousal. I was dumbfounded when I realized that Irene meant to keep love alive with perfume. Worse, if that didn't work, her next ploy was to keep Zachary off guard by flaunting the attention of other men. She would make him jealous.

Luckily, I had learned a thing or two about what keeps people together and knew it had nothing to do with what fragrance she wore or how much she shredded his sense of self-esteem. Elements that hold people together vary in degree. Shared values and goals, the integrity of the family unit, even a dysfunctional one, keep people together. The common denominator of what makes a relationship last is the ability to communicate inner wishes and fears to a responsive partner. In short, not sexual chemistry, but the ability to be intimate.

Historical Perspective on Sexual Detours

A look at history may teach us how the past colors our current attitudes and expectations of love, marriage, and fidelity. In the beginning, sexual detours were not an issue. Cave dwellers didn't hold seminars on strengthening their marriages.

In the history of mankind, sexual intimacy did not begin with fidelity. Male and female met, mated, and separated in the same manner as almost all other animals. Among cave-dwelling humans, monogamy for life did not occur. While sexual activity did not include fidelity, it contained something much more profound: With impregnation of the female, sex left attachment in its wake. Not between lovers, but something much more instinctual: the passionate attachment between mother and child. This attachment, as much a biological imperative as procreation, ensured survival of the species.

In the book *Passionate Attachments*, Willard Gaylin observes that the human infant is born in a state of helplessness unparalleled in the animal kingdom. Babies remain in a state of incapacity, unable to survive, longer than any other creature. The human infant can neither clutch nor cling, nor is it capable of fight or flight. A loving adult must care for it. Imagine that: *must*. Otherwise a baby will soon die.

The need for attachment stems from our upright posture. Our brains are massive, but the pelvis—because it is structured to an upright state—cannot give birth to a fully formed head. We are born prematurely. The first year of life is an extrauterine fetal year. The attachment between mother and child gives the infant the best chance to survive not only this premature birth but also the many years ahead.

With the evolution of humans, females of the species gathered together in groups in order to better ensure the survival of their young. The group effort resulted in the evolution of cultivation and storage. Females clustered in shelters that males would visit, then leave. Sex would attract the men. Motherhood would hold the women. It still does.

When agriculture took root, men began to spend more time around these clusters, and groups evolved in which males played a more permanent part. As primitive clans were established, incest taboos developed, but indiscriminate mating remained necessary for survival of the species.

Males and females eventually learned that their family unit increased their ability to survive. Only then did marriage evolve. Marriage existed in the context of procreation. Children were needed to help with the labor that ensured the family's survival. Ages passed where marriage laws and customs were a simple civil ceremony. Only when the Holy Roman Empire and canonical law were at their peak did marriage become a holy sacrament. This enabled families to more securely transfer land and inherit wealth. Marriage choices were largely made on the basis of the wealth the partner could bring into the new family unit. Companionship, happiness, and contentment were held in high regard, but they all existed as lesser considerations. Marriages were an economic matter, an orderly, *arranged* affair.

The Emergence of Courtly Love

Love, however, was another story. In human history, love had been loosely defined either as eros—sexual desire—or as spiritual love. The Greeks considered friendship the purest form of love. Eastern cultures did not burden their relationships, which often showed great warmth, stability, and devotion, with the notion of romantic love. Sexual desire was separate from the notion of love. Love in the context of romantic love did not enter society's vocabulary until the twelfth century. Our Western romantic-love-before-marriage premise is a holdover from the Middle Ages when crusades and troubadours were in full session. During that period in time, the concept of romantic love blossomed, and afterward it became fashionable to marry for *love*.

Courtly love swept through the feudal courts of medieval Europe in a tidal wave of poetry, songs, and love stories that ignited the imagination of the Western world. Its fire, aided in the later eighteenth century by the rise of the pulp novel, blazed a trail into myths that have carried the notion straight down into our present-day hearts. Romantic love—from the Song of Solomon to Shakespeare—became epidemic. Courtly love caught the romantic imagination and filled inner needs to the extent that it has remained a driving force of our present-day relationships. We drink romance as old wine in new glasses.

THE CONNECTION BETWEEN COURTLY LOVE AND ADULTERY

For hundreds of years, "falling in love" was presented as a rupture of the conjugal couple—adultery. History celebrates adultery. In literature and myth, some of the most passionate love affairs occurred when one or both of the lovers were married. Paris and Helen, Tristan and Iseult, Lancelot and Guinevere, Paolo and Francesca, Don Quixote and Dulcinea, Dante and Beatrice, Anthony and Cleopatra.

The phenomenon of romance and courtly love was not left to the imagination. The ladies of the Middle Ages gathered into groups called courts of love. Their purpose was to define the rules and traditions of love. According to *A Short History of Women* by John Langdon-Davies, such a court, led by the Countess of Champagne in May 1174, created a list of thirty-one rules that explicitly defined the rules of romance. A sampling:

Marriage is no good excuse against loving.
Whoever cannot conceal a thing, cannot love.
Love must always grow greater or grow less.
Love that is known publicly rarely lasts.
Every lover turns pale in the sight of the co-lover.
A new lover makes one quit the old.
Real jealousy always increases the worth of love.
The true lover is haunted by the co-lover's image unceasingly.

Extramarital passion was love. Love was yearning. Love was lust. Love was infidelity. We still seek to emulate in an institution of reality—namely, marriage—the forbidden romantic love that existed only in myth.

This then is our legacy: an animal heritage of biological givens that embraces both indiscriminate mating and an instinct for attachment, marriage as an economic survival tool that is no longer necessary, and an eight-hundred-year-old romantic code of love that has little to do with either.

The Contemporary Nature of Sexual Detours

Just as a look at history provides a glimmer of understanding for our present-day attitudes and expectations about love and marriage, a glance at our present-day lives shows us how those past romantic love ideals provide fertile ground for adultery. Romantic love continues to be a loose cannon on the deck of marriage. We only have to look at the growing divorce rate to prove this claim. Affairs are commonplace. Half of marriages end in divorce. More children are raised in shattered families than united ones.

Affairs are present to a great degree in marriages that end in divorce. Affairs are reflections of how we isolate ourselves from our marriage partner. This desire for isolation may stem from the unrealistic expectations we have of our partner, which can result in unspoken resentments, anger, even despair. Given the degree to which affairs contribute to the isolation of marital partners, it is easy to see why a host of misconceptions have accumulated about affairs.

Four Misconceptions About Affairs

1. *In every affair there is a saint and a sinner; the victim is a saint and the betrayer a sinner.* It is not as simple as that. An affair is not something that happens *to* people. It happens *between* two people, even though one may have been betrayed.

   Notwithstanding cruelty and abuse, both marital partners have a piece of the pie of responsibility when one partner chooses a sexual detour. We may or may not have acknowledged our role consciously, but there are no victims, only volunteers. Sadly, affairs turn love into alienation more often than enduring friendship, and moral judgments have no constructive force. They do not heal wounds or shattered families.

2. *The marriage is over.* Clearly, that is not the case. An affair is not something that ends marriages. Period. I'll say it again: An affair is the cover story. The real drama lies in the underlying factors within ourselves and how they manifest in a relationship. It takes two people to form a marital relationship. Or fail at forming one.

   An affair, if understood at its deepest level, can help a marriage. A marriage where one or both of the partners have unexpressed and unmet needs is not a marriage where intimacy exists. What we learn about ourselves on a sexual detour and are able to integrate into our lives may enrich and strengthen our marriage. When an affair ends, a real marriage may actually begin.

Many marriages begin with intimacy but lose it somewhere along the way. In an attempt to find it again, we may look for intimacy in an affair. Intimacy, however, is not baggage we transfer from one place to another or one relationship to another. It is built step by step. In forgoing an attempt to rebuild intimacy within a marriage by looking for it in an affair, we forgo the potential intimacy that marriage may have to offer.

3. *Sex in the marriage has failed and is over.*

> Sex does not fail, communication does.
> Sex in affairs can exist without love.
> Sex is not intimacy.
> Sex cannot resolve and heal the past.
> Sex is not a substitute for low self-esteem.
> Sex can be restored.

We are sexual beings capable of having multiple sexual partners. Intimacy is another story. We rarely have several intimate relationships. Intimate relationships are not easily substituted. A marriage that has undergone the challenge of surviving a sexual detour can be successful in every way. Intimacy can be established. Sex can become an expression of the intimacy the relationship did not have before.

4. *An affair means we no longer love our spouse.* An affair does not reflect on love as much as it does on our ability to understand ourselves or communicate with another. Affairs mean different things to different people.

In order to shatter myths, it is easier to recognize what an affair is *not*:

> An affair is not the end of the world.
> Nor is it the beginning.
> An affair is not something to be afraid of.
> An affair is not about receiving a new lease on life.
> An affair is not the answer to our prayers.
> And contrary to how those of us caught up in the rapture may feel, it's not even the realization of our wildest dreams.
> An affair has nothing to do with more, or better, sex.
> An affair is not even about betrayal.
> Certainly not sin.
> An affair has nothing to do with love.
> An affair is not about a younger body or better-looking face.
> It has nothing to do with beautiful eyes, or more hair, or great legs.
> Most important, an affair is not even about somebody else. It has nothing to do with who is in your arms. It has to do with what is going on inside.

An affair is an urgent message written in code about what's going on inside of us. As an example, let's use Jake.

Jake has been married for thirteen years. Jake is a hardworking, earnest man, with a rich creative streak that has been buried under the everydayness of his life and the demands of his career. He adores his children and loves his wife. But. He becomes animated when he talks about the woman with whom he has begun an affair. He can hardly contain his enthusiasm as he describes her. Her eyebrows are gorgeous. They arch. He sighs with adoration. He rhapsodizes. He enthuses about her hair. It lifts off her head. It bounces. Another poignant sigh.

"That's only hair!" I want to bellow at him. And I do. Usually I'm more gentle in translating the bulletins from within. I'm in on what's underneath all the nonsense about the hair. I am the observer, the therapist, and as such, I don't need to fool myself. Jake does. He is defending himself against the pain, fear, and unfulfilled longings of the primitive emotions within his inner world. It's too painful for Jake to see his lost dreams. It's easier to find new ones in someone else's image, someone else's hair, than to undertake the work of making real life better. It is hard for anyone to acknowledge the emptiness inside and bear the terrible isolation of not having a part of one's inner self connected to life.

The truth is that the bounce, the youthfulness of that bounce, brings out something in Jake. Something alive, creative, and vibrant that he doesn't give himself permission to express otherwise. He needs to confront his buried youth, his hopes, his dreams, not her hair. It's never the hair. Or the bounce. Or anything. It's never about somebody else. It's always about ourselves.

The emotions lent by an affair are never given for keeps. Eventually, the bounce will become meaningless. We can continue changing partners all we want—an endless list—given our biological heritage of scouting eyes and vagrant heart. But the problems never change. Only by discovering and feeling what is in our inner

world can we achieve the intimacy we crave. Without this understanding, we will unknowingly be driven toward a sexual detour.

About This Book

In the effort to embolden my patients to take real constructive
action, instead of hiding in denial and wasting their life on mean-
dering detours, I guide them on a voyage of discovery. I encourage
them to pay attention to the region of themselves that lies silent but
that fuels some of the most dramatic choices of our lives. I repair
cables of communication and translate the language of an inner
world so that my patients can become intimate with themselves.
This self-intimacy helps them to emerge integrated and whole, find
who they truly are, and grow empowered to shape the future in a
direct and straightforward manner.

For this reason, I welcome the siren call of a sexual detour. I
implore, beg, and otherwise harangue those patients of mine connected to an affair to harken to its sound, for an affair has a voice all its
own. Unmistakably loud and clear. A voice from within. It is an emotional narrative about ourselves, not just about our marriages. It is a
plea beseeching us to discover our true self and the untapped potential of who we are.

I have tried to put this endeavor into the pages of this book.
This book is of interest to *anyone* connected to a sexual detour:

> Those of us enchanted by the beginning of an affair.
> Those who are in the full throes of an affair.
> Those entangled in an ongoing affair they don't know
> how to end.

Some may want to renew and strengthen an existing marriage.

Others may have come to the painful recognition that an affair means their marriage has come to an end.

Those facing the task of remarriage with the partner in an affair.

Still more meeting the challenge of rebuilding an independent life, without the partner in the affair *or* in the marriage.

And there are those recovering from devastation and injury, living with feelings of betrayal, loss, and abandonment.

This book examines the intrapsychic and interpersonal complexities that lead to a sexual detour, detail what occurs when a sexual detour takes place, and sift through the aftermath to lead you toward recovery. The progression follows the stories of various sexual detours that illustrate how the fantasy and illusion of affairs cover up the real issues we have to recognize in order to make our lives and marriages more rewarding.

Through understanding what a sexual detour means in a very personal way, we can gain a more authentic self. Self-authenticity empowers us with confidence and self-esteem and enables us to express ourselves more easily, bond with others, and risk being vulnerable. Being authentic, we are capable of intimacy, the most positive result of which may be to enrich and strengthen an existing good marriage, end a bad one, or provide for an intimate and lasting relationship with another.

For both men and women, to look inward honestly, to face the inner self intrapsychically and interpersonally, is a heroic journey. Olympian. To know who we really are, to be intimate, takes courage. Joseph Campbell believed that a hero's journey was not contained in a single courageous act but in a life lived in self-discovery. With this book I offer my hand both symbolically and literally to help you embark on your journey within. Because, yes, there is more than a detour to follow.

So, this book contains what I see. It's about what I do. Every day. I bring sight and sound to my patients by guiding them on a voyage of self-discovery. I help them grow whole and become everything they can become. And now I attempt to do the same for you. If I am successful you will be introduced to someone with whom you can become truly intimate: yourself.

So let's get down to business and take a look at ourselves. A good look.

Chapter Two

❦❧

The Self

Know Thyself

—TEMPLE AT DELPHI

"Know thyself?" If I knew myself, I'd run away.

—GOETHE

❧ Some of my patients would swear that I couldn't care less about what they think. They know it's because so much of what they think is designed to bury and deny what they *feel*.

In my office, I tend to use volume. I love to see feelings. I'm desperate for passion. Sadly, I see pain. I see anguish and the terrible isolation people feel because they cannot connect on an inner level with who they really are. So I like it when I see feelings, when my patients know something on a gut level, because it's the inside breaking out. It's the fragile yet indomitable inner self breaking through the eggshell of who we think we are, or who we may even pretend to be.

There's a lot of language floating around trying to explain the self in esoteric, inexplicable terms. But let me make it simple. Who

and what are we talking about when we use the term *self*? We are
who we think we are and feel we are. We are our attitudes and experiences. We are how others experience us. We are a combination of
our thoughts, feelings, and actions. We are a psychological finger-
print of hopes and longings, wishes and fears, that mingle with our
DNA heritage of chemicals and physical and hormonal circuitry.

From the moment of conception, our psychic landscape is
colored in an endless array of hues. With the genetic wiring in
place, this landscape is brought to life at birth, then subjected to
the nurturing process. Our psyche gets woven into the tapestry of
who we are and who we become with a combination of nature
and nurture.

The Unconscious

In thinking about ourselves, it may help to use the example of a
building. Imagine that we exist as the structure of a building. This
building fills up with the content of who we are. The content is a
combination of cognitive thoughts, moods and feelings, actions and
behavior, all influenced by chemicals, genetics, and nurturing.

As in most structures, the basement is the most neglected part.
It seems the least important is left the most unattended. No one
pays attention to it, or wants to visit, let alone live there. The basement houses the equipment that keeps the building running. What
goes on in the basement keeps us functioning: passionate, creative,
alive.

This basement is our unconscious—a storehouse of unremem-
bered frustrations and feelings and events. The thousand and one
acts, events, attitudes, and incidents that we as children experience.

These experiences either helped build and create a good sense of self, or left us fragile and sometimes shattered. These events are put out of our awareness, tucked neatly into the basement.

The basement houses what we record—which is everything. We sift through it in a creative way, submerging pain and anxiety below awareness and allowing only certain feelings to surface. How we feel about ourselves is influenced by that part of ourselves of which we are unaware—the unconscious.

Everything that enters the unconscious during our developmental years stays there. Forever. The unconscious knows no passage of time. The unconscious cannot be taught. It cannot be changed. What is unconscious is an imprint that stays with us. The unconscious part of ourselves never forgets. The unconscious will not be tricked into revealing what lies there. It surfaces in dreams and in our behavior but is often disguised.

Unconscious Dimensions of the Self

One of my patients looked and behaved like a physical metaphor for the unconscious. She was an iceberg. She was majestic and cold. Her haughty arctic beauty froze any human contact. She floated above her inner world in a cool and otherworldly fashion. What she revealed, both to herself and to me, was only the tip of the iceberg. Her icy demeanor and cold control over a tiny and visible portion of herself swam above a submerged continent—a self of which she was unaware. I had the sense that if she didn't map her subterranean depths, she would collide with the forces in the continent and fracture just like ice.

At that time in my practice, I was operating under the impatience of youth, and rather than allow the patient to come to her own conclusions, I impetuously barged ahead. I still operate in this rather charged, headlong fashion because life is too precious to waste one moment in self-absorption rather than self-discovery. Discovery, as I know it, is done by traveling. Movement. In this vein, I bombarded her defenses, feeling that if she was going to crack it might as well be in my office. The rewards were surprising and heartwarming.

She blossomed before my eyes. As it turned out, her ability to recognize and access the hidden parts of herself prevented emotional catastrophe. Instead, she was a natural-born traveler of inner space. The reflection of her inner world began to cast light and color like a prism, an emotional aurora borealis that took one's breath away. She became so much more than an iceberg, as the unconscious dimensions of herself were understood.

UNCONSCIOUS CHOICE

We're all icebergs. A portion of who we are rises above the waterline of conscious sight, but more accumulates below. Knowledge of our depths is vital. The dimensions of what composes that hidden, unknown part of ourselves can rule the day. The importance doesn't lie in the tip. What happens below the surface gives us the power of choice and action, to shape and influence the course of our lives.

What fills our thoughts every day is conscious. If asked, we wax eloquently about who we are. We can be accurate and articulate about ourselves. We have rational explanations of our identity, especially of our behavior, no matter how irrational it may be. However, unless we delve into ourselves and try to understand the motives for our behavior, we will be subject to the influence of events we have suppressed from early in childhood. We will not have the free choice of action in our adulthood.

UNDERSTANDING THE UNCONSCIOUS

Historically, the only way to see into the unconscious has been through free association. It is a wonderful luxury to allow the mind to roam free, unrestrained by structured conscious thought. Einstein discovered the Theory of Relativity using this technique. In free association, or self-association as I like to call it, we do not defend ourselves against the unconscious terror or anxiety within. We are free to see ourselves through the oblique angle of self-interpretation, which, while deadly accurate, is not dead-on.

In interpreting the unconscious dimension of ourselves, we must use intuition, perception, imagination, and metaphor as a way of seeing and understanding. The unconscious refuses to discuss anything in plain English. Symbolic interpretation, for instance, is what we do in order to understand our dreams.

If we view ourselves through the prism of the unconscious, we catch a glimpse of who we are and what we need. This insight gives us freedom to choose what we do on a conscious level, instead of being driven by unconscious forces.

When we are able to see aspects of our unconsciously motivated behavior or feelings, the revelation is, quite simply, surprising. Emotional vision can engender profound epiphanies. Illumination, however, does not need to be earth-shattering at all. Take something as simple as the phenomenon of sudden knowledge. We feel blue, then it strikes us that it's the anniversary of something powerful, like a parent's death or the end of our marriage. The unconscious timetable is never late. These are times of our lives that we buried, but our mood doesn't forget. These events are indelible imprints on our soul. These little lightbulbs are only the daily change of the unconscious part of ourselves. They give us, if we want to accept them, small gifts of self-knowledge. Tokens for the ride.

THE UNCONSCIOUS AT WORK

We all have the habit of avoiding our unconscious subterranean depths and concentrating only on the tip of the iceberg. Something much more fundamental is at work down below, but it's far easier to take the cover story at face value. Take, as an example, this prelude to an affair.

Sam was flirting. He denied it, of course. But he was lunching. A lot. What he was hung up on, what he wanted to resolve in his treatment with me was his dissatisfaction about his wife's looks. Her nose, to be exact. He was stuck on that nose. Why wouldn't she have her nose fixed? She wouldn't listen to him. He tried to persuade, cajole, and plead. If she fixed her nose, everything would be perfect. She would be perfect. He'd even give up lunching.

The nose was nonsense, just like the hair a few pages ago. It wasn't the nose. It's never the nose. One day Sam and I spoke at length about what his feelings about her nose engendered in him and tried to discover if it reminded him of anything significant in his early life. When he connected his wife's nose to his past, he bolted upright, as if struck by lightning. The more he talked about his feelings as the son of a critical, selfish, disapproving father—a dad who didn't seem to care how he felt, who never gave the little kid or gawky adolescent enough approval to feel good about himself—the less his wife's looks mattered. The more he talked about how bad he felt about himself, the better he felt about his wife's nose.

Soon the nose lay by the wayside. A pretty nose became unimportant in the context of why his wife's looks were so important to him. It became clear that he was fixated on his wife's looks, but his unconscious was fixed on his father's disapproval. Her looks had been carrying the burden of his self-esteem, serving the function of receiving approval from the world and from his father. A big job for one imperfect nose.

Trying to escape from feeling a certain way about himself, as his father's son, via the detour of his wife's fixed nose—or an affair with someone more attractive—would have been a dead end for Sam. Sam could have obsessed over appearances all he wanted. Plastic surgery on his wife's nose wouldn't ever change how he felt about himself. He would have bounced from nose to legs, from stomach to breasts; from lunch to dinner. There's no end in sight. Only the recognition of what lurked beneath the surface would ever have given Sam, or his wife, a breather. It's backbreaking work trying to shore up unconscious issues of self-esteem by fixing someone else's nose.

We can change ourselves. What we cannot do is change the past or someone else. It's never about someone else. It's always about ourselves. My point is that if we concentrate on the cover story of an affair, we do so at our own peril. We allow the real drama to go unrecognized. These dramas are internal issues from an earlier day, stored in the basement of the self, that may motivate us to go on a sexual detour without even knowing the real reason why.

Nurturing and Self-Esteem

Growing up is hardly a benign process. None of us escapes the glory or the heartbreak inherent in childhood. Indeed, our sense of ourselves and self-worth is always well-trodden ground. We all sustain the footprints of those who have stomped, unwittingly and usually lovingly, on the garden of our budding self (and there are many of us blighted blossoms floating around the world). The inevitable stampede of parenting guarantees that we will sustain bruises.

The painful events of childhood become a tender spot we avoid by suppression or denial. The area of conflict—the bruise—camouflages pain in much the same way a bump develops a black-and-blue shield. We literally drop painful events into the unconscious, where they remain out of our awareness. These become our unmet, unconscious needs and to our knowledge don't exist. But they do exist—in the way they are expressed in adult relationships. With our intimate adult partners, we seek to have these wounds healed and, in doing so, inadvertently create more conflict because our unconscious expectations are supremely unrealistic.

We develop good self-esteem from a mothering experience that recognizes our true wishes and shows us approval, not rejection. The nurturing process of childhood can enhance or diminish how we feel about who we are. While our physical bodies depend upon physical nurturing, our identity develops through intimate personal nurturing with our mothering figure. With a nurturing mother, who can accept us for who we are, a whole sense of ourselves flourishes. We grow into authentic, creative, confident adults, capable of intimacy. Sounds easy. It's not. Parents, too, are flawed human beings.

Sometimes, our sense of ourselves is compromised because our emotional needs were not met. If the handling is a bit rough, we do not develop an authentic, whole sense of who we are. We may even develop a false self. This is our camouflaged representation to the world of how we had to be seen as a child. When we have had the kind of mothering that does not reflect our true emotional state, does not approve of it, or overrules it in an effort to fill our mother's own needs, we learn to reject ourselves. Our experience with another parenting figure, like the father, can mitigate a negative effect, but the younger we are, the more indelible this imprint of disapproval from the mothering figure. Our self-esteem is at the mercy of our first romance.

OUR FIRST ROMANCE

What takes place during the nurturing process, during our first romance, is crucial to our adult relationships because there is a direct connection between this experience and a later capacity for intimacy and love. The first romance predicts the nature of every other romance. Fathers, siblings, life experiences, too, all color and impact the building of the concept of ourselves, but when our first relationship is traumatic it will leave a slight fissure in our self-esteem. Consequently, problems with how we feel about ourselves come forward later in life and hinder developing an intimate relationship in adulthood.

One of the deepest needs, beginning with infancy, is for acceptance and approval. But somewhere along the road, some of us learn that if we share something truly important to us, it is devalued, taken away, or not even noticed. We feel frustrated, misunderstood, and invalidated. If we are known for who we are and still gain approval, we develop an authentic sense of self. If not, we are compromised and wounded, and the repair job is left to us in our adulthood. This is the repair job we may mistakenly and unknowingly seek by going on a sexual detour. This is the drama we conceal with the cover story of an affair.

The Development of Sexuality

The development of sexuality is a further extension of childhood self-esteem issues. The integration of ourselves as sexual beings begins in infancy with a bath of physical sensations that are crucial to survival. In infancy, physical and emotional bliss merge. We seek to reexperience this union in an adult sexual relationship. The adult wish to have a partner who kisses, smiles, and holds the same way we experienced in infancy is built on familiarity. It is what we have stored in our unconscious memory. When the kind of touch we received as infants is not congruent with the kind of touch we receive in our adult relationships, some adjusting is required. For example, a lack of touch in infancy might lead to a greater need in adulthood, but it may be a need we find difficulty expressing because we've never had the experience to duplicate. Conversely, a physically affectionate mothering experience might leave us unfulfilled with a less demonstrative mate in adulthood.

The relationship between intimate sexual adults can be compared, in its intensity, only to the love between mothers and babies. The baby relates to the mother using her body as well as its own. The reason our adolescent and adult relationships are so intense is that they reawaken in our unconscious world the first passionate attachment of our first romance.

Sexuality is the adult physical expression of all we have experienced before. Sex can soothe and bring many sources of anxiety under control, as did a mother's holding, stroking, soothing, and comforting. Aside from the instinctual biological urge, sexual union provides a mutual sense of caring for the adult just as nurturing in early infancy did for the infant.

THE WORLD OF SEXUAL MATURITY

We make giant strides from the sexuality of infancy and childhood to the sexual maturity of adulthood. We move at lightning speed. The baby moves from playing with the mother to playing with himself. We crawl toward a separate physical self, all the while building closer emotional ties to help weather the psychic journey ahead. Our early growth is a precursor of the seeming paradox of adult relationships, where intimacy requires that we are separate and connected at the same time.

So it goes that after the intimacy and bliss of infancy and childhood, we're treated to what may appear to be a handful of relatively calm years in an innocent, latent childhood, where we are sane, manageable short people. This theater of operations is a staging ground for adolescence, where the needs that are later expressed in sexuality mull around, preparing for the real invasion. When puberty bursts upon the scene, it hits us with a tidal wave of hormones. Flooded by growth, and sexual capabilities, we are catapulted into the adult world, sexual organs leading the way.

The sexual maturity of adolescence thrusts upon us the complex world of adult sexual relationships before we are emotionally ready. We emerge from adolescence lustful creatures full of insane desire, longing for the reunion and passionate attachment of our first romance. And before we know it, we're there. From mother's arms to lover's arms. We sail on wings woven in an earlier time, sustained in flight by cloth spun of unconscious longings and dreams. Hopefully, we're well on our way toward being a whole, integrated, and authentic self. Usually we're not. But we're in the thick of it. And how do we try to recapture that first romance and replay our earliest drama? We do it, of course, by falling in love.

Chapter Three

Romantic Love

Lovers come. And lovers go. Over the sands of time
they go. And they know all there is to know.
Lovers know.

—KORAN

Love looks not with the eyes, but with the mind,
And therefore is winged Cupid painted blind.

—SHAKESPEARE,

A MIDSUMMER NIGHT'S DREAM

*It had to be you . . . In this world of ordinary people . . . Some
enchanted evening . . .* Anyone who remembers Broadway musicals,
or has been entranced by the golden era of movies, knows about
romantic love. Knows it by sight, by sound, and by heart. We all
have the same expectations of romantic love. It will be intense and
rapturous, and last forever.

Freud taught that all love is a refinding. Psychology abounds
with the theme that in romantic love we attempt to re-create the
bliss and union of infancy. Perhaps even more than the recapturing,

we want to make it last. Romantic love, at its deepest level, is about hope. It is a wish for the reunion of that first romance. Nothing demonstrates more poignantly the intensity of that inner longing for reunion than love at first sight. And it happens. It really does. And forgive me for being the messenger, but romantic love dies. If we are to have forever after, and all that the hope in romantic love wants to achieve, we have to learn how to find it by creating intimacy, but we won't have it with romantic love. I'll say it again: Romantic love fades. And here's why.

Romantic love is a complexity of unconscious, involuntary feelings, attitudes, and expectations about love. "In lust" happens at first sight, and we call it love. We idealize. The passion of romance is always directed at our own expectations, our own fantasies. To fall in love, according to Stendhal, one must first admire, then fantasize, receive a shred of hope followed by a dollop of doubt. The doubt creates a line of tension that gives us both pleasure and anxiety.

Romantic Love Is Our Idealization

Let's get something straight: As pure, innocent, sweet, and cherishable as it is, romantic love is blind. Deaf and dumb as well. This is another thing I hound my patients about. They protect their beloved from my prying eyes because they know what I will see. I will not see the same person they do—the person they wish existed. This can work conversely; sometimes what I see is a lot rosier than what out-of-love jaundiced eyes see. But I press my point even to deaf, love-struck ears.

LOVE AT FIRST SIGHT

In love at first sight, the other person doesn't even have to be there. Whom we see, whom we meet, even whom we fall in love with has little to do with the other person. Even the one standing right in front of us. People "fall in love" with images. Lovers are replications of pictures tucked way back in the realm of unconscious memory. We all yearn and seek, find and re-create. We idealize people as we did the parents of our childhood. The image of the parent stamped upon our souls is never far from romantic love's eyes. The complication is that the same trigger that generates romantic love also conjures up memories of disappointment, separation, loss, and abandonment. Sooner or later this ambivalent mixture of love and disappointment surfaces. There are always two sides to every coin.

Love at first sight is triggered by the unconscious memory of something overwhelmingly positive and familiar. In what has been called the recognition of love, we hear a haunting melody, something we once knew. One trait or another in the desired person sets off an instant regeneration of the primary parent. It could be the shadow of a smile, but it's enough to set the wheels in motion. That flash of recognition triggers our imagination and creates our ideal. Consequently, what we see in the beloved is deadly accurate. Those rose-colored glasses are prescription lenses geared for the wearer.

LOVE AS THE WISH FOR SYMBOLIC UNION

Falling in love is a longing. Everyone knows that, above all else, lovers want to be together. The earliest myths spoke directly of union and reunion. Plato comprehended the nature of romantic love. In Aristophanes' myth, as portrayed in Plato's *Symposium,* primordial man was round with four hands and four feet. He had a single head with two faces on a swivel neck. When the creature dared challenge the gods, Zeus punished him by cutting him in two. But once man was split, each half yearned for the other. Zeus, in pity, moved their reproductive organs in order that they could periodically fit together.

> For the intense yearning which each of them has towards the other does not appear to be the desire of lover's inter-course, but of something else which the soul of either evidently desires but cannot tell, and of which she has only a dark and doubtful presentiment. Suppose Hephaestus, with his instruments, to come to the pair who are lying side by side and to say to them . . . "Do you desire to be wholly one, always day and night to be in one another's company? For if this is what you desire I am ready to melt you into one and let you grow together.". . .There is not a man of them who when he heard the proposal would deny . . . that this meeting and melting into one another, this becoming one instead of two, was the very expression of his ancient need.*

Two and a half millennia have passed since this was written. With the emergence of psychology, we have gained insight into the intensity of the mother-infant relationship and now more fully understand what Plato meant by "ancient need."

---

* Plato, *The Symposium: The Benjamin Jowett Translation* (New York: Modern Library, 1996).

The Evolution of Romantic Love

The notion of romance as we know it today burst into Western society during the Middle Ages with a tale of love and death. Romance made its debut with two of the most famous lovers of all time, Tristan and Iseult. Adulterous lovers. Their story, as in all romantic love, carries a theme of separation and longing for reunion. The moving, epic tale of the star-crossed lovers' saga imprinted itself upon the entire Western world a mere eight hundred years ago and created the tide of romanticism upon which we still ride today.

I have paraphrased here the story of Tristan and Iseult, so magnificently retold and explored by Robert A. Johnson in his book *We: Understanding the Psychology of Romantic Love,* in order to illustrate romantic love and how it still colors our emotional lives today.

Tristan was destined to become a great Knight. Iseult, the Fair Daughter of Sorcery, had the gift of healing. She was beautiful and desirable beyond measure. She was destined to become a Queen.

When Tristan is wounded in a battle, only Iseult can save him. Tristan is taken to Iseult for healing and, upon recovery, returns to serve the King. A bird drops a strand of golden hair. The King, taken by the bright gold hair, vows to wed the woman to whom the strand belongs. Tristan offers to find her, for he had recognized the strand of hair as belonging to Iseult.

Tristan finds Iseult and takes her to his King. Iseult's mother gives Iseult a wedding night love potion designed to cast a magic spell on Iseult and the King. Iseult and Tristan mistakenly drink this potion on the voyage. Drunk with the magical spell of the love potion, Tristan and Iseult spend one night together. When they reach the King's land, Iseult marries the King and becomes Queen. The lovers, still under the spell of the love potion, are miserable apart. They come together in an enchanted orchard, outside of time and reality, and live there together. After a period of years, filled with honorable intentions to serve the King, Tristan and Iseult separate and return to reality.

Tristan, despite marrying another, remains possessed by Iseult. Iseult longs for Tristan. Tortured by separation, Tristan vows to return. When Tristan's wife learns of her husband's longing for Iseult and his plan to reunite with her, she takes vengeance upon him by deceiving him into thinking that Iseult has died. Believing his beloved Iseult dead, Tristan dies of grief. Iseult, upon finding him so, dies from sorrow by his side.

Oh, my. Who doesn't love lovers? The whole world loves lovers. And who doesn't want what they have? We all do. Only it's easier to have in myth than in reality. Friendship can live. Love can grow. Sex can get better. Mature love can endure. Intimacy can last. But romantic love dies because we outlive the idealistic state of the enchanted orchard.

THE THREE CHARACTERISTICS OF ROMANTIC LOVE

The early notions of romantic love, and the falling-in-love state that characterized courtly love, exhibited three characteristics all designed to fan the flames of desire and keep romantic love alive.

1. Because romantic love began as a taboo, the first requirement was that the lovers were not sexually involved. This
was eventually modified.
2. The second requirement was that the lovers were married to others.
3. The third requirement encouraged the lovers to suffer
from intense desire.

In order to sustain this intensity, passion was never exposed to
the everydayness of marriage. Separation heightened passion.
Contact and confrontation were thought to unravel illusion. Ardor
was kept alive by being stoked, not slaked. Beyond illusion, passion relied on another key ingredient: mystery. Romantic love was
more akin to idealization and worship.

In myth, intense romantic love is short-lived. It often ends,
tragically, in death. We've mixed a good deal of this romantic love
into sex, into marriage, and into "forever after." We've re-created
what Tristan and Iseult had for a scant few years but try to stretch it
into lasting forever. We still hold the medieval belief that true love
is the ecstatic adoration of an image of perfection. Only in our
imagination can such an ideal exist. In myth, romantic love is
clearly defined. In real life, love, sex, marriage, and intimacy are far
more complicated and confusing.

We must draw a line between the euphoria of romantic love
and the reality of creating intimacy. Romantic love actually inhibits
intimacy because romance is based on illusion, and intimacy is
founded on reality. Marriage helps create intimacy but inhibits
romance. Familiarity, certainty, predictability, and repetition
destroy the illusion of romantic love, but these characteristics help
us build an enduring and enriching life. Intimacy can follow roman-

tic love but should not be confused with it. If we believe that only romantic love will provide intimacy, we delude and shortchange ourselves. Intimacy alone can fulfill what that longing for romantic union represents.

The Chemistry of Love

So romantic love walks in, and what do we have? First, a flash of memory. A primitive unconscious recognition that triggers the creative genius of our imagination. The creative imagination has immense power. Romantic love eludes conscious directives primarily because it is such an unconsciously driven state. The phenomenon releases a storm of chemicals and hormones that nothing on earth can stop. These chemicals, in league with the unconscious, are invincible. Romantic love is a concoction of attraction and attachment dependent upon the potent mix of chemicals.

Romantic love has two stages: attraction and attachment. The eyes serve as portals for attraction. Chemistry, as far as we know, begins visually. The hormones overwhelm us with a hormonal cocktail that results in a physical and emotional state of love and attachment.

ATTRACTION

Conscious—and unconscious—recognition triggers attraction. This releases three hormones—natural amphetamines: phenylethylamine (PEA), dopamine, and norepinephrine. Voilà, we have a love potion.

This heady chemical mix for passion, not unlike the love potion of Tristan and Iseult, is designed to last just about as long, two to three years. That is the life expectancy of romantic love and, interestingly enough, also an affair. Attraction begun visually is a physical state: The chemical basis puts the body on red alert. Joy and excitement mingle with apprehension and anxiety. This feeling resembles fear. Our body finds itself in a state of constant readiness. Our heart beats faster, our mouth gets dry, our palms sweat. The chemicals course through our bodies, giving us a bright-eyed fervor that probably has more to do with survival than love.

The attraction phase coincides with infatuation or what is known as idealization of the love object. When love occurs, we become extraordinary people. The beloved is endowed with power, and the lover basks in the reflected glow. Our self-worth is bound up in the beloved, just as it was in our first romance. Romantic love allows the lover to feel more attractive. Mutual romantic love creates self-validation, a love chorus wherein lovers confirm each other's worth in a timeless duet.

ATTACHMENT

The second part of romantic love is a physical bond of attachment. This begins after the brain stops giving off signals for the love potion. The PEA hormone of the romantic love potion, with its amphetaminelike high, triggers an alarm. After the PEA, the brain sends messages for the endorphins to calm the frenzy. Endorphins are more peaceful, tranquil substances. One of the hormones in this calming phase is oxytocin, produced by the pituitary gland and described as a "cuddle drug." This hormone may be present in higher levels in long-term love. Oxytocin is found in exceptionally high levels in prairie voles, a rodent family known for its rigid monogamy.

When the endorphins take charge, the PEA falls and we settle into the attachment phase of mating so that child rearing can take place. On the evolutionary scale it has rationale. In order to ensure survival of the species, a hormonal mix had to bring about mating, then reduce the desire for sex in order to allow time for the mother to raise the infant. This attachment phase lasts long enough for a toddler to learn to walk. When the mother is free to care for a new baby, the cycle begins again, and the evolutionary engine is jump-started once more. Should our eyes fall on a likely subject, we are once again flooded with PEA and another frenzy of mating can occur. And so the story (and survival of the species) goes.

Romantic Love as an Escape

Adolescents fall in love very easily. The more mature we are, the more difficult it is to fall heedlessly in love. That in and of itself is not a bad thing. Sometimes the highway of romantic love is a detour, in much the same way as a sexual affair. Many people distract themselves from the real growth of adulthood that still lies ahead by the headlong plunge into romantic love. Romantic love can deter us from the challenge of self-development when we submerge our interests and goals and jump into idealized relationships that might not be in our best interest.

In summary, as adults, we try to obtain from our lover what we did not receive from our parents. It is not possible to be in love without reinvoking old conflicts that cause us to re-create an ambivalent relationship. Consequently, we try to resolve past childhood conflicts in a new context with adult partners. The intensity of this relationship represents a window of opportunity for inner knowledge and repair—but we must walk this tightrope carefully. Romantic love can rewrite the drama of our lives and, in many ways, can be a force for change and growth. Or, if we are not aware of its distracting influence, romantic love can deter us from growth and change.

Romantic love makes us terribly vulnerable because we idealize the other and invest him or her with such importance. The refinding of the other, as an adult, becomes so important that we become determined to take possession of what we have recaptured with the ultimate step of commitment.

In this state, shaped by life situations and societal influences, under the influence of unconscious wishes and sustaining the greatest hormonal storm since puberty, we drink of the love potion. Drunk, under the powerful heat of sex, under the sway of the moon and the stars, and with all the hope and yearning romantic love can arouse. You guessed it. We pledge our troth. Like Tristan and Iseult, we vow to forsake all others. In myth, this is where the romance is enshrined in immortality as one or both of the lovers die. In reality, we get married.

Chapter Four

❧ ❧

Marriage

Man is a knot, a web, a mesh, into which
relationships are tied.

—ANTOINE DE SAINT-EXUPÉRY

❧ Marriage. Rings and things, symbols and celebration. It is a joyous time of life. I cry at weddings. Who doesn't? But why do we cry? Perhaps we cry at the unbearable beauty, the innocence and the fragility of hope. Perhaps we cry because journeys end in lovers meeting. We cry at reunion. Or perhaps we cry because what we find at the end of the journey, the long road home, is so cherished yet so fragile.

All lovers exist in their own private Eden, like Tristan and Iseult, blind to the world around them. But unlike the enchanted orchard of romantic love, marriage is a public affair. Reality is a witness. In the eyes of God, or the State, when we take our lifelong vows, the world watches. We find ourselves down the road from that first romance with an adult version. For better or worse, until death do us part. We find ourselves married.

Embarking on marriage, we all soar, we sail. It is a time of life when emotions run high. Dreams. Expectations. Few of us recognize how fully in marriage we are bound to touch earth. In the midst of euphoria, just below the shimmering surface, swim the undercurrents of fear. Anxiety lurks furtively, like an uninvited guest at the celebration. To one degree or another, we harbor doubts, fears. The future seems to present itself with surprising suddenness. We face the unknown. What lies ahead is new. Terrifyingly new.

We marry, brimming with hope for a future, not even hearing the echoes of the past. But deep within resonates something very old. Inextricably woven in with the new, as yet unknown to us, the past has already been introduced; it has already taken hold. All, or part, of what we have chosen in marriage represents the resurrection of old patterns. We have chosen, in our new life, with a new wife or new husband, something very familiar. In marriage, this fact is revealed to us in surprising ways.

The Wish for Married Bliss

What we unconsciously strive for is someone to help us fill the emptiness. We yearn and long for the feeling of that first romance. Whether we had it and want to recapture it, or never had it and seek to fulfill it, we long for union. For bliss.

Not to disparage the notion, but for many, bliss is synonymous with the kind of union difficult to maintain in the real world. I treated a couple in premarital therapy who believed that, in order to be wedded, they had to be literally joined. The two independent, strong-minded individuals, who had come to me to hash out the decision to marry, were already chafing at the restrictions their expectations had built into their forthcoming marriage. They sat and stared at me, eyes glazed over, and sick smiles pasted on their faces as if their collars had suddenly become too tight. Fortunately, they couldn't convince me that their new favorite word was *we*.

They equated married bliss with an extreme kind of togetherness. They were going to drown each other in their misguided attempt and were submerged in a sea of false expectations. I worried that this would doom them to an early divorce. I released them from their expectations when I balked as one of them was going to accompany the other to the bathroom. I hollered that they could pee together if they wanted to, as long as it wasn't in my office. Bladder functioning notwithstanding, they were eventually able to take delight in the fact that they were two separate people, each respecting and valuing the differences between them as much as their common ground. To this day, twenty-odd years later, they still value and hold this concept dear.

The Sexual Highway

Whom we choose to marry, and why, can be revealed only by the language of the inner self. What we look for in marriage, and what all the legacy of romantic love represents, is a replay of that drama we already know that is tucked away in the unconscious part of the self. All the longings, all the needs, and all the wants left unattended cry out for attention in marriage. A sexual highway forms in the marital relationship that links the past to the present. The sexual marital relationship literally provides a connection from the everyday life of the present to the psychic life of the past. Marriage becomes a two-way street allowing passage for the conflicts from the past to emerge. A free subway ride from the past into the present.

Marriage, as the most intimate relationship we can form in adulthood, forces us to deal with the most formidable issues of our early self. In our marriage, we struggle with issues left over from the development of ourselves in an earlier time. Despite the conflicts marriage presents, it is still the best place for us to try to work out having a lasting, intimate, loving relationship. It's far from easy. As one patient reminded me, any two people can live together as long as they like; only marriage partners face the daunting task of staying together as long as they live.

Intimacy in marriage requires that we have an integrated self. Whole. That we have the ability to move beyond the fantasy, beyond the illusion of romantic love, and form an intimate relationship with another. Besides having realistic expectations, it requires us to have an inner dialogue about who we are and allows us to reveal that self to another. Our issues of the past pursue us from the sexual highway into marriage. If we have a wounded or shattered sense of self, it will interfere with our capacity for intimacy.

There are two main arenas of emotional conflict. The first is the fear of intimacy as represented by two sides of the same emotional coin: abandonment, and control. The second is transference.

FEAR OF INTIMACY

Two seemingly opposite sets of emotions interfere with intimacy: abandonment, and control. At their root, they are the same in that both occur in individuals with a fragile sense of self-esteem, yet at first glance they appear strikingly dissimilar.

Fear of abandonment and fear of control are both sides of the same coin: fear of intimacy. They cannot be felt at the same time. Usually we feel more of one side of the coin than the other. Sometimes we choose a person who expresses the opposite side of this coin for us. I see this in many couples. The adage that opposites attract only means we are similar underneath. I see people with a fear of abandonment pick someone with a fear of control, so one can run and the other can chase. They engage in a duet wherein each person replays past conflicts and expresses fear of intimacy in his or her own unique way.

Fear of Abandonment

A fear of abandonment makes us feel as if we will die or disappear without the other person. As if we will lose ourselves. As infants, this feeling occurred when we lost sight of our mother, because we were not yet able to take care of ourselves and being alone threatened survival. This feeling is so terrible that we may seek to avoid feeling it ever again. Even in adulthood, when being alone does not threaten survival, we may feel as if it does.

When we fear abandonment, we may try to stay glued onto another. We may seek to preserve the illusion of intimacy but, in truth, maintain a distance that prevents us from the vulnerability of intimacy. We may never develop ourselves as independent, whole individuals. Instead of dealing with the fear that we won't be able to survive, we try to avoid the feeling entirely.

Jill's fear of abandonment pushed her to choose men with one foot out the door. She assured me that this was not because she didn't want intimacy. She explained time and again that, most of all, she wanted a commitment. I knew that what she said was true. I also knew that on an unconscious level this wasn't true. She was simply repeating a drama within and avoiding the creation of a new life story for herself.

Unconsciously, Jill chose relationships that created distance and abandonment because that was all she had ever known. Like all of us, she tried to change the past by choosing someone in the present and then trying to change that person so she wouldn't feel the loss and abandonment. Like a broken record, she held onto the past, trying to change history by choosing unavailable men who she hoped would change and become available to her at last. She kept picking all the unavailable men she could find. The more unattainable they were, the more she ran after them, tried to hold them. And, of course, she lost them. She continued to try to change the father of the past by choosing someone like him in the present.

I wanted to convey to Jill that her behavior was designed to maintain distance. She was only repeating unconscious patterns. She would never have to risk being in a relationship if she kept choosing men who would leave. She could continue to be rejected, as she had been by her abandoning father, and keep trying to change the past by repeating it, or she could confront herself and create a new future. In order to do so, she would have to allow herself to feel abandonment and loss and see that she could survive.

I convinced Jill to make a very conscious decision as opposed to following her unconscious pattern. I told her to go against her grain. I suggested that she do an end run around her unconscious compulsion to repeat the past and now pick an available man. A truly available man. Then make it work. She resisted, of course, and thought I was batty, but I badgered until she took a risk and tried, and then tried harder and kept trying. And then of course we both cried at her wedding.

Fear of Control

Fear of control occurs when intimacy feels controlling. Commitment issues are frequent manifestations of this fear because we equate being close to someone with being engulfed by him or her and losing ourselves. We don't want to get too close because something that is frightening or anxiety-producing is associated with closeness. The reason we fear being "smothered" or "swallowed up" by another is that we have a fragile sense of ourselves and perceive the other person as overwhelming and dangerous. The root feeling is—again—that we won't be able to survive.

Paul had a fear of intimacy that manifested itself in an inability to commit. In his early forties, he had never formed a lasting relationship. He stayed in a relationship only as long as he was the one chasing. He thought he fell in love too easily, but I knew the real problem was that he couldn't allow himself to love at all. He fell in love with fantasy, and as soon as the true person and the demands of an actual relationship surfaced, he fell out of love. As soon as real intimacy was offered, he felt threatened.

When Paul was in his chaser syndrome, he would smile at me gleefully, as if to show he had no issue with intimacy. His excuse was always the same. It was his girlfriend who wouldn't hold still and commit to a relationship. I chided him because I knew that he chose people who wouldn't commit because *he* couldn't. As long as they could be blamed, he didn't have to confront himself. He and I both knew he didn't have a snowball's chance in Havana of having a lasting relationship with his current flame. A girl who was halfway out the door was a perfect choice for him. As perfect as the last one had been, and the one before her. Chasing was always a perfect way to avoid the challenge intimacy posed.

As long as the woman was unattainable, Paul loved her. He

didn't want to digest the fact that this was the only way he felt safe enough to move toward a woman. The moment a woman turned toward him, he backed away. They all had to appear aloof, unattainable, in order for Paul to stay and move closer. When the women stopped running, which invariably they did, Paul's chasing would come to a screeching halt and he would run the other way.

Many times Paul has voiced the fear that he would be caught. If it wasn't *caught*, it was *controlled. Strangled. Swallowed.* He worried that he would lose himself if he got married. I helped him see that being in a relationship did not mean regressing into the control of a critical and overpowering mother. But Paul carries his negative mother inside, so he still has a weak sense of himself, avoiding intimacy with another in order to avoid her.

Paul outruns his fears by constantly engaging in go-nowhere affairs because the infantile fear of not being able to survive overwhelms him. It will require Paul's conscious decision to change his behavior if he wants a real relationship. He will have to force himself to stand still and negotiate the delicate act of merging into a relationship with someone. When he does, he may find he can be in a relationship yet still maintain a sense of who he is and survive. But he has to want that for any real change to take place.

THE EMOTIONAL BAGGAGE OF TRANSFERENCE

The biggest trunk of emotional baggage we carry with us into marriage contains transference. Transference carries past conflicts down the sexual highway and thwarts intimacy because it interferes with our being able to perceive our mate as separate and distinct from the people in our developmental past. To achieve intimacy in marriage, it is crucial that we have the ability to perceive our partners as they really are, not as characters in the dramas taking place within us. We each want to be valued for who we really are, not as a figment of someone else's imagination.

The journey that has taken us to the altar is a unique one. Up until this point, we are each distinct. Getting married requires the creation of a new reality. Marriage is a dramatic act in which two perfect strangers come together hoping to find a new world. What they find is a bit more than what meets the eye. First of all, they have to contend with the group. Six or more to a bed, to be exact. Parents, and assorted others, are all thrashing around between the sheets. It has been said that we meet at the altar, virtual strangers, suffering from one or another delusional state, pledging our troth, promising to love, honor, and cherish forever, accompanied by a host of internal ghosts.

What interferes with our ability to see and respect each other as separate and distinct is the fact that we are blinded by the ghosts of the past and our unconscious wishes. We marry someone, then turn that person into a past figure, usually a mother or father, in order to re-create our earlier story. The force behind our choice of a marriage mate, and how we interact with him or her in a marital relationship, lies in the phenomenon we call transference.

Transference takes place in all relationships, but most dramatically comes into play in the marital relationship. A clever trick of the emotional imagination puts someone from the past, usually a parent figure, onto the face of our marital partner in the present. Our unconscious wiring cuts grooves, like a record, and we want to keep playing the same music over and over again. The people we pick for this replay of past history are those with whom we are intensely involved in the present.

Another way to understand the phenomenon of transference,

both positive and negative, is to see it as a mistake. Many psychologists refer to transference as an error in time. We take feelings we had about people in the past and transfer them to people in the present. All of our feelings, the entire drama, have been perfectly preserved in the unconscious. Our feelings toward our parents are always ambivalent. This means that we resurrect in marriage all the old frustrations and hatreds, as well as the positive feelings. What is frequently sought out in a mate, and is then fought out with that mate, is an unresolved drama with our parents. Some of us do this so well that we never really leave home even when our address changes to one a continent away.

Joe and I are having a debate about the wild ride he is currently on. After five years of marriage, the issue for him became sex. Joe is a stud with Carlotta, the woman with whom he is having an affair, but not with Yvonne, his wife. It's not marriage or his wife that denies Joe the freedom to express himself sexually, although that's what he thinks. He feels that marriage, and in particular Yvonne, has inhibited his sexuality. Why? Because he married his mother. Joe's deeply religious and domineering mother took care of his every need, including handpicking his wife.

Joe can be sexual with Carlotta because she exists outside of the marital reality and the unconscious phenomenon of transference. He has not—yet—cast the mother robes Yvonne currently wears onto Carlotta. Should his wife be removed from the equation, Carlotta would inherit the mantle of Joe's unconscious conflicts about his mother. Yvonne would be free and long gone, and Joe would find himself with old, and new, problems. But that is our ongoing debate. I believe in Joe's sexuality and the ability to enjoy sex within the context of a committed relationship. And if I have it my way, Joe will soon believe that as well and be free to enjoy married sex.

That basement of the self-structure, the unconscious, remembers everything and learns nothing. Once we pull the trigger and transference goes to work, it doesn't matter to whom we are married. All of the past unconscious needs of the self will be layered onto that new person in the present. Our new wife or new husband will do just fine for our purposes, and we will do fine for his or hers. The trouble with this arrangement is that we end up married to the parents we carry around in our heads.

It may seem as if romantic love undergoes a dramatic shift when marriage takes place. What really takes place is that the unconscious feelings are finally free to escape. We have less fear of losing the relationship.

An old adage is that we marry to heal old wounds and settle old scores. All of the unfinished business of our past gets played out with a new partner in the present. There is no way to outfox what psychologists call the repetition compulsion of the unconscious to repeat our past. The unconscious part of the self has simple aspirations. Nothing fancy. The unconscious wants to keep on replaying the same story in an attempt to fix things. As if a switch were left on. Who we are and what we want are bound up in this internal drama. This is the story we must come to know, because it is the driving force behind a sexual detour.

The power of the unconscious lies in our continuing attempt to repeat. The unconscious, as the repository of our past, is the container of the unmet needs of the self. The unconscious uses the present to try to change the past. The unconscious wants to change the past by redoing it in the present. We want to recapture. We want to remake. We want what we had in the past—the bliss part. And we want to redo the pain part, too. We try to change history.

The trouble is that this is futile. We cannot change the past, only try to shape the future.

Knowing the inner self in an intimate way is the only way we can override the repetition compulsion of the unconscious. Self-knowledge doesn't erase the program—transference doesn't disappear—but the power of the unconscious is deflated once it becomes conscious. Consciousness gives us the power of choice. Awareness allows us to create a future instead of just trying to re-create the past.

Stages of Marriage

Most of us marry with unrealistic expectations, unreasonable ideals, and mythological beliefs. We seek safety in marriage and regard it as a harbor, a safe haven in which to live and raise a family. We marry because of tradition, because it is expected, because we cannot fathom life in an unattached state. We marry because of lifestyle, financial support, and appearances. We marry because romantic love and sexual desire swamp us. We marry with variations on a theme, but it is always with the internal wish for the reunion, the refinding of a love object that harkens back to our first passionate connection in life.

When legal marriage takes place, the crucial content of the marriage contract is never revealed. Nothing in the marriage certificate even closely approximates what takes place in our heads. We rarely discuss these assumptions in detail. But the assumptions are there. All of our assumptions about fidelity, discretion, honesty, and how we meet each other's needs is spelled out in clear detail in our unconscious expectations.

The marital agreement we drag around in the unconscious part of our self carries all the specifications of what we expect of our partner. This has nothing to do with our stated objectives or those late-night discussions of what marriage means, of what we expect, or what we intend. Or even of what we are supposed to provide in turn. All our unconscious assumptions were written long, long ago, when the world of the self was very new. Most of the expectations and assumptions begin the same way:

> *If you loved me, you would . . .*
> put the lid down.
> leave the lid up.
> put the cap on.
> leave the cap off.
> walk the dog.
> get rid of the cat.
> turn the music up.
> turn the music down.
> not talk so much.
> talk more.
> want sex all the time.
> not want sex all the time.
> never feel angry, hurt, or misunderstood.
> never let me feel angry, hurt, or misunderstood.

In other words, *make me feel loved, whole. Be perfect for me. Make me perfect, too.*

Somewhere along the way, sooner or later, we find out that marriage means something far different from what our assumptions thought marriage meant. Moreover, it doesn't mean the same thing to our partner as it does to us. Even within our own adult developmental cycle, what marriage means will change. Marriage is a complex tapestry woven of many threads that go back in time. Moreover, how we change over time causes us to create many marriages out of what began as one. There are broad categories common to most marriages. Close behind Shakespeare's seven stages of man, marriage has six stages, each with piercing characteristics lasting around five years, give or take. Marriage is a difficult process to navigate, and having a road map indicating the bumps and curves telling us what to expect is helpful.

STAGE 1: NEWLY MARRIED

We all know this one. It still glistens. It has the musical score. It's the honeymoon phase. We're madly in love. Lots of eye contact, lots of touching. Lots of sex. You are mine. I am yours. You are perfect. I am perfect. We are perfect. We are one.

We experience this stage of marriage more as an expectation than a relationship. It is filled with desire for fusion and contains assumptions, high hopes. The burden we put on our partner in this stage of a relationship is that he or she will make our lives whole, happy, meaningful, intense, and ecstatic. Forever. We have an underlying anxiety about how to make this stage last.

STAGE 2: RECENTLY MARRIED

We attempt to harmonize our married state as we deal with issues of intimacy. In this stage, partners still want fusion but may experience fear of control or fear of abandonment. We begin to recognize that we are not exactly alike. The demands of reality reveal themselves more clearly than before. We notice differences. Different temperaments. Different needs. Annoying characteristics surface.

This phase ends when we recognize that the other is not perfect. Reluctantly, we give up romantic ideas of fusion and perfection as we start to deal with the issues of compromise and settle for what reality has to offer.

Most affairs and divorces occur during the first and second stages of marriage.

STAGE 3: MARRIED

Reality makes itself more deeply known, and handling ambivalence within the relationship becomes important. This stage sets in when expectations begin to assert themselves. We lay to rest our wishes for fusion and settle for a basic merger. *How much of myself do I have to give up to be in a relationship?* We recognize the need for problem-solving skills and master the art of compromise as the pressure of marriage and career combine with the realities of raising a family. Children bring a new reality. We learn that the train of romantic love must exist on a different timetable and track from the one carrying the kids, for the simple reason that a train can't run on two tracks at the same time.

STAGE 4: REALLY MARRIED

This hallmarks the first real recognition of the passage of time. The dramatic changes that accompany growing children and the added responsibilities of parenthood reflect the deepening realities to which a marital relationship is subjected. The need to maintain one's identity is strongly felt and causes conflict. *Who am I? What do I want? Don't want? What do I need? Don't need? What have I become?* Disenchantment with oneself may travel under the guise of disappointment with the partner in marriage.

Sex in this stage of marriage is a lived-in reality with children and family. The juggling doesn't stop there. We are caught between two worlds. Grown children leave home; the parental generation ages and dies. There is little room left for illusion. The turbulence felt at the end of this stage of marriage heralds the oncoming force of change.

Over a quarter of affairs and divorces occur in marriages of fifteen years or more.

STAGE 5: REMARRIED

This time of life is all about change. Changes abound, and with them, a chance for reconciliation presents itself. When children become young adults and leave the family home, there is a mandate for renewal, and the marital relationship changes.

A renewed thrust is present regarding accomplishment in careers. Second careers begin. We see ourselves more clearly and can recognize our own inner struggles. Along with a need for acceptance of oneself and our aging process comes an acceptance of our partner. There is a wish to experience our lives more fully. The sexual relationship often improves when children are away at school and the marriage partners are alone.

STAGE 6: FINALLY MARRIED

A great deal of warmth, acceptance, affection, and tolerance underscore the late stage of marriage. Maturity allows for the inclusion of flaws. The age in which we live prolongs life, vigor, sexuality, and emotional well-being. Redirected energies are aimed at finding out what lies ahead, before what is left is over. We may face the illness or death of a spouse. There are more memories upon which to draw for strength, in contrast to the wishings and longings of earlier times.

Intimacy and Marriage

Ultimately, marriage is not about romantic love. Marriage is not about longing or wanting. Marriage is about having. About giving. About knowing. About seeing and being seen. About hearing and being heard. Marriage is about developing intimacy, the only thing that gives us what all that longing is really about.

Marriage can help us evolve and become more mature, or it can perpetuate the way we seek to isolate ourselves from intimacy. The way we develop intimacy with our self and our partner, and the way we penetrate the veil of transference, is primarily dependent upon the kind of communication system we have developed.

Great sexual feasts do not provide the intimacy necessary to keep a marriage alive. Steamy sex may not survive reality. Sex in marriage has the power to enhance and hold, to allow a real relationship and true intimacy to develop and flourish. But if there is a problem within, where we avoid ourselves, there is a lack of intimacy in the marriage, and eventually this reflects itself in one way or another.

Marriage can become a way of maintaining distance and perpetuating the way we isolate ourselves from intimacy. Not all relationships can withstand intimacy. For those of us with a fragile sense of self, marriage may include an affair that creates the distance we need. The closer we are to another's vulnerabilities, wishes, and fears, the nearer we are to our own. For some of us, real intimacy proves too dangerous, too overwhelming, and we turn away, toward paths that provide more distance.

In search of the intimacy a marriage has not provided, for any number of reasons, we may seek to fill unmet, unspoken needs with an affair. When we do not know what we need, we have difficulty developing a binding tie. In the absence of intimacy, and with the decline of romantic love, under the stress of the realities imposed by one or another stage of married life, the fracture of fidelity can easily occur.

When marriage disappoints, when what we sought to have and hold eludes our grasp, when our attempt at redoing our first romance fails, a shattered self takes flight and seeks to fill unmet needs in other ways. We make a second pass at recapturing that early first romance. We do it silently, quietly, perhaps unknowingly. Even unintentionally. In search of the self we do not yet know or fully feel, we turn away from marriage toward a sexual detour.

PART TWO

Intermezzo

Chapter Five

❧❧

The Triangle

*So heavy is the chain of wedlock that it needs two
to carry it, and sometimes three.*

—ALEXANDRE DUMAS

❧ Flirtation has endless possibilities. Fantasy and illusion cavort rather heedlessly on those grounds. But when we reduce the possibilities to one, we cross the line of seduction. Moments, hours, days, or months may go by before we finally abandon ourselves and cross the threshold. But when we do, when we commit adultery, the innocence of the marriage dies. And somewhere within lies the terrible knowledge that things will never, ever be the same.

When we enter the hidden world of the affair, the laws of the universe, as we know them, cease to exist. Time never again resumes its usual cadence. On a sexual detour, we hover in the half-light of physical reality and emotional fantasy. There, triangles form, reflecting an inner life we have yet to explore or fully understand.

In this hidden world of the sexual detour, there is even a subtle change in climate. The weather of secrets prevails. The secret is as crucial to the existence of this hidden world of the affair as are air and water to the planet we inhabit. Here, whispers float in air that suddenly grows heavier. A silence descends to muffle the sound of reality. Stillness emanates from the secret, weaving a cocoon for the fantasy life of the affair. Affairs live and thrive in this cocoon, where wishes and dreams take form and shape as if to prepare for flight.

Functions of a Secret

The affair is a secret triangle that serves many functions. It lures those of us who are afraid to know who we really are or who we may become. It beckons to those with low self-esteem. The secret of an affair feels safer to those of us who do not feel whole. With a fragile self, we allow ourselves to behave more freely in an affair than in our real lives. The secret affair becomes a private testing ground, before integrating into real life, for a particular action or way of being.

For some, the secrecy of an affair feels like a safer arena for the expression of sexual needs. While sex with a marital partner may be technically good, the sexually charged air of a new and different sexual partner brings fantasies to life and allows us to act them out. It may be easier to reveal our desires without consequence, and attain them without cost, when we act on them secretly. Because it isn't for real. Or for keeps. Marital partners, with the help of transference, often inherit the powerful mantle of parental figures. So instead of learning how to act out sexual fantasies with our spouse, from whom we may fear disapproval, we use the illicit playmate to experiment more freely. In secrecy, we do what children normally do. We misbehave.

Denial in the Affair

The affair stays alive best in secrecy. This keeps the sexual detour safe because it creates denial. An affair is a fragile, furtive thing, designed to serve a fragile self. Secrecy provides cover for the psychic issues within ourselves that we want to keep clamped down, hidden. It is as if the darkness of a secret protects us from seeing or feeling something within ourselves.

This secret releases a peculiar energy. I remember watching Joan pack twice as much into a day as others could in a week during the secrecy of her affair. She moved at lightning speed. She juggled the daily tasks of raising a family with seemingly great ease. Housework, driving a carpool, attending soccer practice and ballet rehearsals, working at her job, and spending time with her husband and lover seemed to go without a hitch. Watching her do life in double time, I knew of course that the frenzy outside masked an even greater frenzy within.

In the absence of external chaos, I sensed that Joan would feel the internal frenzy from which she was so desperately trying to escape. On a sexual detour, she did not have to face inner anxieties or frustrations because the affair offered escape. I could see that Joan's worry over details, about overt lies, was easier to tolerate than the tension of her inner feelings. All the dangers facing Joan seemed to lie in truth, in discovery. I knew that her affair was not a cure and would never heal, only hide.

The Secret Exchange

Marriage is a two-party system. A dramatic change occurs when a third party (a lover) is introduced into a two-party system. On an emotional level, betrayal takes place when secrets are shared. Momentary affairs, purely physical sex that do not contain shared secrets, are far less damaging to marriages. For most people, the ultimate betrayal is not the physical act but the rupture of emotional trust, the sharing of secrets with another.

Often, the distinction that enables many spouses to stay put and help the marriage survive a sexual detour is the belief that blindfolded sex took place. As if no other person were present. An activity more on the order of masturbation. No emotional boundary violations. And very often, it is true that no confidence has been broken. No secrets shared.

A couple came to me with their hearts in their eyes. Frank, the husband, had had a short affair. What should they do? Did this mean something terrible about their marriage?

When Frank described his sexual indiscretions, it was fairly clear to me, as well as to his wife, that his loyalty had remained intact. His trucker's drive-through route had become a few one-night stopovers. There, he availed himself of all the comforts of home. On the blue plate special, sex was served after dinner and secrets were kept, not shared. What I told them to do was to go home and hold each other tightly, hang onto what they had. To forget about his drive-throughs and keep their lives intact. For them, blindfolded sex had indeed taken place and no one else was involved. They could deal with the sexual temptation, the lapse in judgment. For them, no secrets shared meant that no betrayal had taken place.

In another case, Ginny felt distraught not by the sexual act but by how enormously betrayed she felt. She came to see me in a panic and rage. She was crazed. She had been told everything in excruciating detail. Her husband had revealed that he had shared all their secrets. He had told his secret lover Ginny's anguish over their marriage, even her struggle with weight. Their secret rituals had been incorporated into the affair. His betrayal ran deep. Her wounds, therefore, were deeper as well. What she was reacting to was her intimate life being taken away and given to someone else.

Ed had been my patient long before his affair began. His emotional relationship with his wife had always been bare bones. A prisoner's meal. It was watery, thin gruel, barely enough to sustain him. He longed for a rich emotional meal. Despite my efforts at encouraging therapy for them both, his wife remained isolated from any help and unable to join him in the way he wished. When he began his affair, I had a hunch that it was going to bring about the definitive end to his marriage. Not because of any wild sex, but because new secrets were being shared. New life was taking shape and carrying him far beyond the boundaries of his marriage.

Ed and his lover were both architects. They were partners in a design contest. They huddled incessantly, whispering and colluding, forming the alliance he wanted so dearly and had never been able to form with his wife. His betrayal was not in sharing secrets but in forming new ones outside the marriage.

AFFAIRS UNLEASH EMOTIONAL DYNAMITE

Affairs include all types of emotional betrayals in varying degrees. The triangle, when found out, lets loose some of the most powerful, rage-filled emotions of mankind. Emotional dynamite has been set and lit. Betrayal touches on our most primitive, archaic emotions. Helen, whose face launched a thousand ships, was the wife of the king of Sparta. She was abducted by Paris, son of the king of Troy. Homer immortalized the ensuing ten-year Trojan war in the *Iliad* four hundred years later. As I said, lots of dynamite.

Paradoxically, while we unconsciously try to avoid trouble by going on a sexual detour, we end up with more trouble. When problems exist, we may feel left with only two alternatives, either one of which may be dangerous:

1. Deal with problems in the marriage by confronting the painful issues intrapsychically as well as interpersonally and begin the work of resolving them; in other words, improve the marriage.

or

2. End the marriage.

This do-or-die mandate of couplehood is lifted by the introduction of a third party. What is acute becomes chronic. An affair prevents the dissatisfied partner from having to face either one of the two fearful alternatives because it presents a third alternative and another way of having needs met.

The Dynamic of the Triangle

When the third party enters a two-party relationship, the new geometry of love becomes a triangle. An invisible third party is brought into the sexual arena. This third party is never the primary relationship but is the indicator of trouble in the primary relationship. An affair may become the primary relation once the marriage ends, and this is what we fear when a partner has an affair.

From the point of view of the psychology of a relationship, a triangle is a manifestation of a problem *within* the marriage. Something has gone awry in the way the two people interact. One, or both, partner is experiencing painful issues *within*—notice I did not say painful issues *because* of the marriage—and has chosen an alternate way of dealing with the problem. These issues are both intrapersonal and interpersonal.

Whereas intrapersonal has to do with what goes on inside ourselves, interpersonal refers to the business of what goes on between two people. From this interrelationship point of view, emotional triangles are an extension of the primary relationship and are introduced when a two-party system is in trouble.

A triangle introduces distance. It prevents complete intimacy with either the marriage partner or the partner in the affair. It prevents us from having to face internal issues. In marriage, for intimacy to exist, resolution of intrapersonal and interpersonal issues is linked together. In a triangle, the issues of the self and the issues of the relationship are kept wedged apart.

Problems in relationships always have a leg in the individual issues of the past and a leg in the relationship issues of the present. As a practical reality, nothing can stay in this overstretched position for very long. Intimacy bridges the gap between the two worlds. When intimacy fails to exist, we introduce a third person, like a third leg, to relieve the strain on the emotional back of the marriage.

For the marriage, a triangle most often worsens and complicates the relationship. Again, the universal language of the triangle as a tool comes into play. The stable nature of the tripod prevents toppling, and the problem remains unsolved. The very existence of the affair temporarily relieves the tension of internal issues and the problems manifested in the marital relationship. The triangle lessens the intensity of the primary conflict felt within and reduces the interplay of the couple. Conflict is obscured by the third party, because the triangle introduces illusion instead of the coping mechanisms that can realistically solve problems. Triangles, which prevent the system from dissolving, also prevent it from improving. The eventual fault lies in the very nature of the balance, where nothing gets better, nothing gets worse. The triangle obscures personal issues and hampers efforts toward resolution. What the triangle accomplishes best is to waste time. The introduction of a third person delays the imperative to face issues and find solutions.

Eventually, when the affair is discovered, the marriage likely will end. Sixty-five percent of marriages faced with infidelity cannot weather the storm, not only because of the internal issues that interfered with intimacy in the first place but also because the anguish of betrayal carries with it a terrible cost. Far too few of us know how to breach the break in fidelity and heal the wound that betrayal inflicts.

LIFE EXPECTANCY OF A TRIANGLE

The end of an affair lies in its beginning. An affair is a desperate search for stasis, but nothing remains unchanged forever. Affairs are fated for an early death. They usually last two to four years. If the affair becomes public, it is doomed. Reality eventually takes its toll on the affair. If the affair replaces the primary relationship, it is subject to the same emotional stresses and forces as the marriage but is twice as likely to fracture.

Conversely, although an affair survives best in secrecy, the very clandestine nature of the relationship kills it. An affair prevents binding ties from forming. Eventually the affair has nowhere to go, no way to grow. There is nothing of the stuff upon which relationships thrive and survive. Sooner or later affairs die of isolation. They suffocate in the secrecy. Affairs die for the same reason marriages suffer in the first place, only sooner: lack of intimacy.

THE OEDIPAL TRIANGLE

Often the issues that start affairs have to do with Oedipal feelings. The re-creation of this family triangle is so unique, with so many versions; the variations are endless. The most common example paints a sweeping picture of a young, single woman who becomes involved in a relationship of sexual ecstasy with a forbidden, unattainable object: the married man. The eternal triangle replayed.

The term *Oedipal,* which Freud used to describe children's preference for the parent of the opposite sex, comes from the classic myth that plays out in an adult relationship the consequences of a child's wish to overcome the rival and win the parent of the opposite sex. The Oedipal triangle is an erotic one that takes place in all families. Oedipal wishes are sweet and innocent. And very sexualized. At one time or another we all want to be the favored one, the special one. The one who gets to be in Mommy's and Daddy's bed. And we want to do everything they get to do. Everything.

Oedipal fantasies are part of the gas that fuels sexual engines. It is these fantasies that reawaken with a vengeance in puberty and drive masturbation and sexuality. Oedipal feelings are usually abandoned very early because we learn that the gratification of the childhood wish to win a forbidden parent is never granted. These wishes are given up, but the sexual fantasies remain erotically arousing. These kinds of feelings are often replayed in an affair.

Chapter Six

Sexual Detours

> *It is as absurd to say that a man can't love one
> woman all the time as it is to say that a violinist
> needs several violins to play the same music.*
>
> —HONORÉ DE BALZAC

What is surprising is that so many of us, at one time or another, manage to find our way into the hidden world of the affair. Nearly 70 percent of married men and 60 percent of married women have had affairs. Assuming that only one partner in a marriage is involved in an affair, at a minimum, two out of every three marriages are touched by the phenomenal popularity of this seventh sin.

The selection of a partner in a sexual detour is a snap. Lovers are easy to find, far easier than finding a marriage partner. We don't search the world over. It has to do with simple location. The person we have an affair with is almost always right under our nose. It is always someone with whom we have had occasion to become familiar. The reason we don't have to look far is that we're not choosy. In choosing a marriage partner, we work hard, consciously looking for a mate. In the hidden world of the affair, we are being driven by unconscious issues and don't even know we're looking.

Affairs as a Reflection of What We Want to Be

In an affair, we seek a reflection of ourselves as we want to be seen. We look for ourselves in another's eyes. We may not have the self-esteem to feel beautiful. So we seduce a lover and look for validation in another's estimation. We even imagine that we see what we want lying there.

The feelings we have about another person in a secret triangle have more to do with ourselves than with him or her. This is because in an oblique fashion, we look for a part of ourself that we feel missing. Ultimately, the significance of the affair lies in finding out our own identity when we are on a sexual detour. We need to know how to incorporate this new self—the one we like so much—into the real world. This is more important than focusing on whom we are having an affair with. Ridding ourselves, to the extent possible, of denial helps.

Another way we seek to enhance ourselves is by endowing another with the characteristics we wish we had. The person we are with doesn't even need to have everything we're unconsciously seeking. If there is just a smidgen there, we'll flesh it out with the creative power of romantic imagination.

In an affair, we borrow from another what we feel lacking in ourselves: youth, ability, beauty, sexuality, power. This search is camouflaged by the cover story of the affair. Sometimes what we're trying to borrow is as obvious as a cup of sugar. What is the woman with an enormous sense of responsibility looking for in an affair with a carefree, totally irresponsible man? One good guess is a sense of freedom. She wants an escape from the unremitting and unforgiving burden she most likely imposes upon herself.

In affairs we see all sorts of dog-and-pony shows: the collector who has an affair with an artist; the cold, stiff politician who falls for the showgirl along with her bohemian lifestyle; the heiress who runs away with her chauffeur. Age and youth. Beauty and brains. Rich and poor. We've heard the clichés before, because they're tru-isms that exploit the contrast, the differences. Unerringly, we're drawn to what we think we don't own or can't have. We find ele-ments in the partner of an affair that we try on, like costumes in a masquerade, and act out a story uniquely our own.

In fortunate instances, an affair sets free in us something vital, lasting, even though the liaison is temporary. The experience may unleash forces in our personality that remain long after the affair is over. And to the extent that a sexual detour is a catalyst for change, it can be a positive force. Unfortunately, the reverse usually hap-pens. Too often the secret affair is a regressive way of avoiding the real work of change. Rather than becoming, we run away from a marriage and hide in an affair. When this happens we deny our-selves the fulfillment of our own potential.

The Triggers for an Affair

The psychic groundwork for an affair is laid long before marriage, but the trigger for an affair is usually a specific life stress more apt to occur at one particular time of our life than another. Stress decreases our ability to tolerate the frustration of unmet needs and thus increases our vulnerability to the quick fix, the easy escape into ecstasy. The more contact we have with the outside world, the more likely we are to take a sexual detour. This is particularly true if we do not have to account for our time.

We often have affairs when we need a change. Indeed, many have said that the cropping up of romantic love is about being in need of change. Like a catch-22, change also harbors stress. Stress occurs in times of change because there is a need to realign and readjust. Our emotional gears don't always mesh smoothly, much less fit in with someone else's. Specific stresses can lead to affairs. A demotion in a job lowers our self-esteem, and we may look for it elsewhere. A promotion shifts our sense of ourselves the other way around, and may underscore our insecurities and present our vulnerabilities in a new way.

There are various stages during marriage where natural transitions occur, and sometimes, in these stages, the stress leaves us vulnerable to sexual detours.

EARLY YEARS AND CHILDBIRTH

The early years of marriage are volatile. Pregnancy and the birth of a child usually bring partners closer together, but many are also driven farther apart. The fears and responsibilities awakened by parenthood send many scuttling for escape under the covers of an affair.

THE CHILD-REARING YEARS

Many men feel a sense of loss as the wife is taken up with child care. Similarly, the loss of a husband to career leaves many women longing for companionship, and they seek a male who offers friendship and is simply more available.

MIDLIFE

The phase of marriage that midlife partners face is one of the most stressful. Couples confront complex issues that include coming to terms with the loss of their dreams. They face an empty nest as children are launched into their own adulthood.

LATE MIDLIFE

Later midlife brings a perceived loss of sexual desirability. Breasts drooping, hips spreading, business downsizing, Dow falling. We fight against gravity, trying to lift our failing powers of seduction. Men may feel their diminishing power in the external world and assuage themselves by exercising prowess in the sexual realm. And for the fading beauty, the reaffirmation of sexual desirability by having an affair reflects what her mirror no longer does.

Acting out an Affair

Mature adult behavior can tolerate frustration, live more peaceably with unmet needs, and find fulfillment. When we have not developed a whole sense of ourselves, we tend not to be able to withstand any deprivation. We act in ways that are more unruly, unreasonable, and sometimes self-destructive. Adolescent. Technically, having an affair is "acting out." In the language of psychology, this means that what is going on inside, rather than being felt or dealt with, is being displayed in behavior. We are literally acting out what is inside our unconscious world in order to eliminate the negative tension, instead of understanding it and modifying our behavior.

When we do not have a sense of a whole integrated self and cannot tolerate our inner conflicts, we instinctually have a knee-jerk reaction designed to avoid the tension of negative feelings. We must rid ourselves of them. Our unconscious tensions are like thunderheads looming below the horizon of sight, creating an electrical discharge of behavior that often leads to a sexual affair. Psychic lightning.

Acting out is *doing something*, but it is not a consciously understood, planned *something*. A sexual detour is hardly ever a conscious goal or planned activity. The behavior does not fulfill a conscious directive like enrolling in a class or taking a bus to the museum. The doing something is an unconscious attempt to avoid feeling the anxiety of our inner self. It is designed to keep the feelings of unbearable frustration, terror, or anxiety at bay. Sexual acting out is only one small segment of this kind of behavior. Acting out behavior encompasses rage, depression, and all kinds of obsessive-compulsive addictive behavior.

Sexual acting out behavior masks feeling the frustration and anxiety that accompany our inner conflicts. Naturally, when we avoid the issues we fail to come to terms with our problems. The critical feature in adult psychic development, in growing whole, is the ability to deal with our problems in constructive ways. With a whole sense of ourselves, we can more easily tolerate frustration and anxiety and find acceptable solutions.

As a therapist dealing with the internal conflicts that are frequently demonstrated by sexual acting out, I get advance reviews of sexual detours. I'm given a brief outline of the story and then a lot about component parts. I get promo pieces of leading characters, skewed views of the opposition, a line or two about the supporting cast. I get snapshots, posters, and picture postcards advertising the land of lust and longing. I get sound bites about firm flesh slapping against the thighs versus the flabby version. I know about high-hard versus soft-natural. I get reviews that quantify and qualify. But one thing's for sure: Nothing I get approximates what is really going on in the inner world.

It is perhaps an irony that looking at a wedding cake may lend understanding to sexual detours. Like a wedding cake, there are three levels, or tiers, to every affair: The first level, the top tier, is the presenting symbol. It's decorated for allure. It's lovely. Like romantic love, it is also more symbolic than substantial. It consists mostly of frosting. This top tier is the cover story. The sexual detour. The affair.

The second level, the second tier of this cake, represents the marriage and the way the couple interacts. This is the marital relationship. How the couple communicates and builds intimacy is reflected in this level of interrelatedness.

The third level, the bottom tier of the wedding cake, is the least decorated. Not at all beguiling, with hardly any frosting, it doesn't taste as good. This biggest layer is, predictably, the most important layer. It's the foundation for the entire wedding cake. This represents the inner world and the fissures in our feelings about ourselves. What goes on here works its way up and comes out in the second layer. Therapy is about getting into this bottom third level. A good result here helps us deal with what goes on in the second layer and even affects whether or not there is a top tier.

Reasons Behind Affairs

Affairs are a complicated drama, like the characters who play in them. Often, many issues intertwine and touch on one another to form a complicated piece known as an affair. Sometimes it's a simple melody and it's easy to hear one major chord. Sometimes there are multiple issues that combine into more complex entanglements. The following chapters illustrate case histories that point out the predominant feature of what function the sexual affair plays. This function is usually hidden in the cover story of the affair and is the issue the person on the sexual detour wants to avoid. While the reasons for sexual acting out are as unique as the people involved, there are some broad categories that can illustrate how affairs provide cover stories for the conflicts going on within ourselves. The sexual detour may serve different functions for the individual and/or the marriage. Generally speaking, as they pertain to the individual, they are:

- *A search for identity.* Sometimes we look for ourselves in the lives and accomplishments of others. Their lives seem to provide something our own life lacks. Another person's power, beauty, career, or personal attributes are sought to give us a sense of our own identity.
- *An avoidance of profound life issues.* The emotions aroused by a sexual affair may function as the way we deny and distract ourselves in order to mask the terror, anxiety, and chaos of internal conflicts brought about by unresolved life situations or profound events.
- *An escape from anxiety.* Stress is reduced by mastur-

bation or sexual activity. Sexual affairs that take on the nature of obsessive-compulsive behavior fall into the category of an addiction.

☞ A substitute for intimacy. Those who fear abandonment and loss or fear engulfment and control and are uncomfortable with intimacy use sexual behavior as a substitute for emotional intimacy because intimacy provokes fear, and sex is something over which they can feel they have control. Sex, because it is used as an excuse for emotional intimacy, provides distance in the relationship.

☞ A source of self-esteem. Sometimes we look for ourselves in another's eyes. A desirability contest is won with a new sexual partner. For both, an affair may be sought for reassurance or repair in an effort to rebuild damaged or nonexistent self-esteem. Men may assert themselves sexually to combat fears in other, more daunting realms. Women may seek to combat fears of aging with sexual desirability.

☞ A weapon of power. Self-esteem issues are also present here, but there is an underpinning of hostility toward the opposite sex. Sex is used to control, to defend, and to manipulate. Men seek power in the sexual realm, and otherwise powerless women can become overtly seductive. In seduction, both men and women render the opposite sex less powerful and thus by default become more powerful.

☞ A method of sustaining the marriage. An affair may function to sustain the status quo and avoid dealing

with issues in the marriage that necessitate change. The affair allows the marriage to continue when the needs of one or both partners are compartmentalized and fulfillment is sought in other ways.

Chapter Seven

***

Marsha: A Search for Identity

We carry within us the wonders we seek without us.

—SIR THOMAS BROWNE,

RELIGIO MEDICI

Many affairs remind me of a fable called "The Bluebird." In the story, two innocent children look the world over, search heaven and earth, even the realm of death, for the bluebird of happiness. Eventually, they find it right in their own backyard. I like to think this is a metaphor for finding it in themselves.

Identities, like pieces of a jigsaw puzzle, are made up of enough pieces to form a recognizable picture and help us understand who we are. So it is with feeling a whole sense of ourselves. Sometimes when we have little sense of ourselves, we look to another person to provide something rather than look to ourselves to fill the void. Power, beauty, money, status, or even youth—these are all sought as a substitute for a whole sense of self. Inevitably, the disappointment we feel when we cannot find or feel ourselves in that futile search leads us to search elsewhere. Sometimes, we search forever. The following case history demonstrates such a search.

I felt the vitality of Marsha's presence before I even saw her. The deep, rich timbre of her voice carried an energy that crackled on the phone. She requested a double session, so I could get to know her a bit more quickly. Hurriedly, she went on to outline a rather complicated schedule. She was available only here, there, out of town, in town, etc. Could I possibly fit her into one of those windows in time? "Window in time." An apt choice of words, I thought, for someone in a hurry.

We spoke briefly in the shorthand of quick intelligence. The date and time were echoed back to me, accurately memorized. She assured me she wouldn't be late and she needed no directions. Not for a moment had I a doubt of either.

Marsha had an arresting physical charisma. In her mid-forties, she was an attractive woman, even beautiful, in a strongly handsome way. The navy blue of her eyes seemed to intensify as she looked directly at me and took my hand firmly. In reality I'm a small person, but I seem large. In her handshake I felt tiny, in the grip of a powerfully competent woman. I wondered if she felt that way about herself. I didn't know it yet, but the way she experienced her self-identity was as fragile as a house of cards.

Marsha settled herself into the depths of my overstuffed couch, comfortably tucking a leg under her. She glanced around, took in the surroundings, and with a quick nod of approval, smiled at me. Then, as if readying herself for action, she notched some of her hair behind her ear, leaned toward me, and launched into a lively description of her life. She had been married for twenty-odd years to a lawyer. They had met in college, and upon marrying, she had dropped out. He went on to law school, she to raise their family. Their two grown sons were now living away from home.

Marsha was psychologically aware, physically active, and intellectually accomplished but had not availed herself of what a career might have to offer. She had returned to school when her children were young and dabbled in a number of subjects. Over the years, she had held several high-level managerial jobs but felt mainly unknown for her efforts, unrecognized for her talents, and mired down in the bureaucracy of her work.

This theme of being unrecognized extended into her marriage. She felt that her husband looked through her. Past her. He was flirtatious with other women but, to her knowledge, not unfaithful. She knew only that she felt less important than him. Not exactly belittled by him in word or deed, but smaller somehow. She had felt the same way with her father, as if he never really saw her. Her father, too, had been absorbed in his own life, as if he lived it alone. She felt she didn't get credit for being a daughter, as if she mattered less to him than his fatherhood did.

She confided that her marriage seemed perfect to outsiders. Everyone thought they were a terrific couple. "Everyone" included her husband's therapist. Her therapist. Their marital therapist. Even the circle of friends included therapists. So much for therapists, I thought.

Marsha assured me that her problems were not due to lack of psychological insight. She had insight in spades and had availed herself of all the psychological help anyone could possibly want. She had been quite thoroughly analyzed. She'd followed analysis with a number of other therapists. She assured me that sex wasn't a problem. As a young woman, she had always felt sexually attractive and had been sexually active. Her husband was proud of their sexual relationship. But then, she added almost as an afterthought, sex wasn't an issue simply because sex was always good. It had been good with a number of the men with whom she'd had affairs. It was in this way, rather blithely and obliquely, that she revealed the fact of her lovers.

Her husband knew nothing of her affairs. None of these affairs had seriously disrupted the marriage. She wanted clearly to make the point that the problem was chronic. That she had always been searching for something. Someone. Notice it hadn't been for herself.

It was then, with a mixture of somber reflection and luminescent wonder, that she told me what brought her to me. Finally, after twenty-three years of marriage, she had met the right man. I could tell by the breathy sound of her voice and the somewhat reverent air on which her sigh floated that I had to play for time. Her discovery of this person had been such a long time in coming that the pressure beneath the affair was like a gas leak under concrete. It could threaten to blow sky high at any moment. Whether this explosion was right or wrong, good or bad, I could not yet know. I knew only that explosion per se was not good.

I asked her to tell me not about this right man, but about the wrong one. I asked her whom she had been living with for twenty-odd years. She bolted upright, hooting again with hard, long laughter as she stabbed a finger at the region of her heart, ready to implode:

Who? Who? Me. That's who. I've been living with myself.

Even though she had created her husband from collage material, created every inch of their life together, he didn't recognize her great accomplishment, didn't realize who she was. And as for Mr. Finally Right, Marsha exhaled, the implosion staved off for a moment, as she relaxed again:

Leonard is the only one who really sees me.

And that was my first introduction to Leonard, the man who was her partner in an affair. The right man Marsha finally found and loved.

I wanted to learn more, not necessarily about Leonard but about whom it was that Leonard saw. When I pressed her in the ensuing session for *whom* it was Leonard saw, what that person felt like, Marsha could respond only with who *he* was. Leonard had a cachet about him. He was a successful writer, with a long list of publications. He had a glamorous life and an even more glamorous past. Leonard was passionate. Sex was wonderful. They spent long, lazy afternoons making love. Leonard had time to spare. He was in the midst of writer's block. That gave him a lot of time. Leonard was described as a sensitive, deeply insightful person, who confided all his fears. Not at all like Marsha's flimsy husband who was filled with bluster. Leonard had no arrogance. Leonard made her feel needed.

Although Marsha told me she wanted to explore where she was going, I feared she already knew. She was in a hurry. Knowing she had decided, I told her in my general opinion that wherever she was going, it was too fast.

Marsha began seeing more of me, but it was almost as if it were to legitimize and accelerate her pace in the affair. Her husband still knew nothing, even though she wasn't particularly trying to hide anything. We had a tacit understanding that I was trying to put the brakes on a runaway train. She knew I was not content simply to witness her life. I wanted to meddle. I wanted her to slow down, but as the winds of change rushed past my ears, I heard chaos breaking around the corner. I resorted to one of my less subtle ploys: outright shouting.

Are you crazy?! Let's tread water awhile, Marsha.
I'm drowning and you want me to tread water?
Leonard, as dry land, is a dangerous notion. I'm dry land. Here.

In therapy, we like time. We don't want intense emotions to be acted out and discharged with abrupt behavior. We like issues to be tolerated, looked at, understood, and examined long enough perhaps to be modified. Therapy creates an emotional space where intense emotions can exist and be communicated in ways other than in the unconscious knee-jerk reaction of psychic lightning.

Play it in quarter time, I urged. I wanted Marsha to gain more of a picture of how Leonard was allowing her to feel, who it was she thought Leonard saw, in the hope that we would discover who Marsha really was. Because after twenty-three years of living with the wrong man and seeing all the right therapists, Marsha still didn't know all of who she was. She had no real sense of herself. She wasn't whole. She needed to have an identity, not borrow one.

But Marsha was too hot to slow down. Within the month she was leaving. Leonard and Marsha were going to spend three weeks together. Explanations to her husband were vague, reflecting the empty space that filled the marriage. She was going to introduce Leonard to the physical world, teach him how to hike, maybe even ski. Leonard, for his part, was going to introduce her to his three grown daughters.

I remember vividly the session upon Marsha's return, if only for its vibrancy. The leaves were blowing off the trees. It was a glorious, blustery fall day, filled with color, full of action in the sky. I should have taken it as a sign. Marsha blew in, aglow, cheeks ruddy, eyes sparkling. She had met all his girls. Leonard's women. They loved her. She loved them. Everyone loved everyone. She was dying to make them pumpkin pies, lemon tarts. Make their lives festive. Make them a family.

And your own children. What of them?
They'll love Leonard.
Are you going to tell your husband, or just let him find out?
Actually, I've already told him.

I could hear the distant sound of the family fracturing. Like fine old crystal, worn thin by time. But I could see the stars shining in Marsha's eyes, obscuring vision. Feeling the vortex, I held onto the trappings of reality.

To Marsha, for the moment, a whole new world beckoned. Marsha held a vision of what she and Leonard could attain together. Glamour. Success. Leonard offered an alternative to feeling unimportant. His was a world of status, creativity. She felt she could do with him what she was incapable of doing herself. She could fulfill herself. Be whom he saw. What that said to me was that at last she could have an identity.

Marsha's marriage dissolved before my very eyes. It was rather easily accomplished, in a matter of weeks. It is amazing, once the die is cast, how quickly events ensue. True, it was made easier by the fact that their sons had already relocated their lives. True, it was accomplished speedily by the greased exit of Marsha's husband, who soon became involved with another woman. What seemed to affect Marsha the most was selling the family home and dividing up their finances. This shook Marsha to some degree. But Leonard was successful. There was a new life in store.

The divorce brought our sessions to an end. From start to finish it had been barely five months since Marsha had first called.

They were going to stay for several months in Mexico. The enchantment appealed. Serenades beckoned. Leonard could work from there. The new life and new identity were close at hand. In fact, she had a project in mind for the two of them. I felt strangely depressed, not able to taste the optimism that flavored her announcements, feeling I had somehow failed, in that wink of an eye, to help her. And as quickly as she had entered therapy, Marsha left. Flew out that window in time.

From time to time, I received notes from Marsha. They had decided to stay in Mexico for a year. The house was on a piece of land jutting out to sea. Glorious. An announcement of Marsha and Leonard's marriage drifted in like a piece of kelp. Then:

The house up here is too narrow. I feel like I'm in a tunnel.

Space sometimes opens up possibilities within, I thought to myself. Maybe even gets blamed for the lack of potential we feel inside, for what we are restricting ourselves from becoming. Then, nearly a year later, I received a phone call:

Hey, is that window in time still open?

Marsha blew in with the same energy and vitality I remembered. She looked a bit different. She sat in the same at-ready stance, quick to banter and laugh, but a worried look haunted her eyes. The new place, the new start, were new all right. What that translated into was strange. Unfamiliar. Even a past that had not always felt good was familiar.

The realities of her new life rankled. She didn't like being a stepmother to Leonard's daughters. She found them irritating. They drained Leonard of financial resources. He was besotted by their need of him and refused to urge them to become financially independent. The writer's block that had left so much time for sex was taking a toll on her new identity.

The project she had envisioned working on, their debut as a writing team, still hadn't happened. I suggested that perhaps working on her ideas and not waiting for him might be an option. She might discover what she could do without him. She might discover a way of opening up that narrow house.

In time, Marsha gave up Mexico and they returned to California, where Marsha's energy and vitality were poured into real estate. Her search for a new life became an effort to find roots. They purchased a house, which she went to great lengths to restore. But it became painfully obvious that just as she had created the last life looking to her husband for an identity, she was doing it again. The new life with Leonard was beginning to resemble the one she had undone. Away from the rosy glow of the affair and in the glare of marital reality, her new life was beginning to make her feel like her old self.

The house never really became a home. In the ensuing year, the ominous signs that had been there all along became more and more apparent. Leonard's endearing fears became annoying. A chronic depression plagued him, and it became clear he needed her to lift him out of himself. Marsha felt emotionally drained by his depression and dependency on her. She was indeed needed as she had seemed to want, but this was not the new life she had imagined. She had envisioned a team. Now she felt responsible for the dogsled. She felt as if she was hauling the emotional load. She said she felt like a nurse. She wanted a divorce.

The vision that had entranced Marsha, the person she thought Leonard had really seen, was not who she really was. It was who and how *she wanted* to be seen. The affair was a cover story hiding the lack of her own identity and the fact that she was not a super-woman but a person needing to find strength and fulfillment. First the affair, then the marriage, had extended the charade. The affair allowed them both to buy into the smokescreen Marsha represented to the world. A woman in charge, in control, able to do anything and everything. Create lives. Except one of her own.

Marsha began to see and feel her own vulnerabilities and understand the dynamics of what had been the pressure under her divorce and remarriage. She began really to know herself and become whole.

As much as Marsha's insights were a beginning, as much as they helped her grow whole, they ended her marriage to Leonard. Like many relationships born of affairs, the second marriage that had been so hurriedly grasped in fantasy evaporated with reality. So as the winds of change howled fiercely around us, I held on more tightly than ever. Until on a particularly strong gust, I let go. Marsha flew out that window again, this time a bit more whole, and charted a course toward the unknown.

The bulletins still drift in. Home is Manhattan. Marsha went back to school and is finishing her doctorate. She began writing about her own insightful and unique experience of finding herself at such a late stage in life and is looking forward to seeing it published. Now at what is so graciously referred to as a woman of uncertain age, Marsha feels radiant, alive, and well. Peacefully empowered. It was a long journey home. And like the journey we all share, while still containing uncertainty, it is also filled with potential.

Chapter Eight

❧❧

Norma: An Avoidance of a Life Issue

Life is as tedious as a twice-told tale.

—SHAKESPEARE

❧ All sexual affairs are detours of one sort or another. Rather than feel what takes place within the inner world, the acting out behavior provides a cover story. This is seen most clearly when the affair serves as a distraction from a profound life issue. I want to make clear that by distraction I in no way mean to convey a flighty, pleasurable diversion or diminish the emotional power in an affair. Rather, I am trying to convey how a sexual detour can represent an escape from a profound unconscious event we are desperately seeking to deny. We avoid dealing with the enormity of inner conflict by pouring ourselves into the very seductive emotions present in an affair. The problem, of course, is that, in time, the affair ceases to mask the issues. The inner problems that are not faced or resolved resurface.

The case that best illustrates the divergent nature of affairs, the errant deflection that skews and diffracts our consciousness so that we actually stray from the matrimonial path, is shown by

Norma. In her case, the compelling emotional work of dealing with separation and loss was a profound life issue that needed to be undertaken in order for her to move comfortably forward in life. Instead, she flew into fantasy and illusions and buried her emotions in an affair.

The sexual affair, which seemed to provide the romantic dream come true, was an escape from terrors Norma had managed to disguise in many ways until the death of her mother and the separation from her daughters when they left home. The terror of separation then became too great to handle, and Norma escaped facing these feelings by fleeing into an affair. The circuitous attempt to avoid and deny did not last, for in the end a crisis with her beloved grandson served to bring her, as the poet T. S. Eliot wrote, back from where she started. The beginning.

Like perfume, the memory of Norma's story lingers. I was called in during a crisis, when her losses were mounting, to stop the flow, ebb the tide, before she was drained of what she felt to be her lifeblood. I had met Norma fleetingly, through a circle of associates, a decade earlier. I remembered her as a bright, beautiful woman. The appearance of the woman who walked in the door ten years later shocked me. Norma, on the downslope of fifty, seemed greatly aged. She carried a great weight, not just in the excess poundage she had cloaked herself in, but also in her bent head and the look in her eyes.

The acute crisis that precipitated her seeking my help was her daughter's impending divorce. Norma had been the primary mothering figure to her grandson since his birth six years earlier. The custody issues of the divorce meant that she would see less of her grandson. Norma obviously had a deep and passionate connection to him and he to her. She was distraught over the pain he felt and the threat of losing the boy. Her fear and rage about this were ripping the family apart and threatened to tear asunder any remaining ties to her daughter. The seams of Norma's life were coming apart before her eyes, as cover stories often do.

Norma was the only child of elderly immigrants. Norma described great freedom in her childhood. But what this translated into was that Norma had raised herself. She was accustomed to awakening after her parents had left for work, eating breakfast, and taking herself to school and back. By the age of six, she was on her own every day from seven in the morning until just before dark. Norma took care of her parents by taking care of herself. The subtext of loneliness and danger colored her life but was never openly acknowledged. Norma had such denial of her terror that—unfelt and unrecognized—it governed the rest of her life.

At the ripe age of eighteen, feeling twice her age, Norma married a knight complete with shining armor. In quick succession they had two daughters. She felt that her real life had finally begun. Norma marveled at her good fortune: a home, children. What mattered most to Norma was that her children have a mother who was always there. Finally, in becoming the kind of mother she had unconsciously longed for, she had one. She remembered wishing time could stand still.

Then the past intruded. All the fear, all the terror Norma should have been able to feel in her young fragile childhood, she began to feel in her safe and secure adulthood. Soon after the birth of her second daughter, she began to awake in a panic, forgetting where she had put the child, fearing that the children were lost. She picked up the children at school drenched with sweat until she caught sight of them. Relentless, and in pursuit of the past, her unconscious fears tracked her. As her children grew, so did her panic attacks and agoraphobia. Her past was being played out for her in the music of the unconscious, like a record stuck in the same old groove.

Suddenly Norma's father, then her mother, died. The shock left Norma grieving and assuming responsibility for their deaths. Often children of abused childhoods cannot give up the role of taking care of others. But they never learn how to take care of themselves. The burden she had always carried suddenly grew heavier under the full measure of her tremendous guilt.

Within months after the death of her mother, her daughters left to go off to college. Norma remained in shock. They were all gone. Bereft of her attachments, reeling in place, she tried to stand still, to grasp what was already gone. Appalled, she realized that all the ones she had taken care of, all the ones she had given her life to, were no longer there. They had left and taken her life with them. They had left her with the life she had created for them. Like an empty sack.

The issues in Norma's marriage had been shelved in the press of the child-rearing that shaped her life. Although her knight enabled her to create the world she lived in, she lived alone. Her husband lived an interior life, embedded in work. Norma's main sense of an interactive life had come from her children. Norma didn't really foresee that the place that felt so safe, the place she had inhabited as a refuge, mothering, caretaking, was a dangerous place for a shattered self to be.

As is so often the case when children are launched, even when a full, rich marital life exists, and even when a whole sense of self is alive, enormous pressure and stress are put on the system. The marital system that had been established in Norma's case was not able to provide for her unmet inner needs. As is always the case, her marriage was unable to save her from herself. The current life issue of separation and loss evoked inner terrors that mounted until she could no longer handle them and began to act out.

Norma began compulsively to overeat. She gained fifty pounds. In desperation, she sought help. She found a well-known diet guru, a nutritionist. He was charismatic. He paid attention. He listened. It was predictable looking back what would happen next. She looked at me for a moment, hesitating before telling me the story.

You know what happened next, don't you?
Yes. I can guess.

Of course I could. It happens all the time. For the next few years she kept the issues of her terror at separation and loss hidden under the cover story of the affair.

The cover story worked well enough, at first. In the early stages of her affair, Norma shed her weight like a garment. Norma saw an illusion of herself in her lover's eyes that did not resemble the terrified, bereaved, obese woman in the mirror. With him, she could be someone else. She reinvented herself not as a daughter, or wife, or mother. In a hauntingly familiar role, replete with all the fractured pieces of her broken self, Norma's path turned away from feeling her terror, and dealing with it, into an escape. It was so much easier to drown in the emotions of the affair than to feel separation and loss.

Norma filled the empty sack of her life with a new version of reality, one laced with fantasy and romantic illusion. Her terror and grief dried up because, as she told me with an ironic smile, mascara runs if you cry. The affair became the place where she did not get over her terror, guilt, or grief; she simply bypassed it. She dealt with her children leaving home and her mother's death by leaving, too. I smiled at the clever reasoning and the sly tricks the unconscious plays on us. As if we were outfoxing the drama within.

Sex, even though it may stretch like a cat in the overheated, charged air of attraction, is not the primary motivation for many sexual detours. Feeling pain, feeling powerless or alienated, our link to a comforter and ally becomes sexualized and acted upon when change within ourselves might suffice.

Now, the trigger for the terrors that had lain dormant under the avoidance mechanism of being in the affair was the threat of losing her grandson. The current terror of separation and loss resurrected her old terrors. Norma's current distress spoke volumes. Echoes of fear-filled lifelong chords were not difficult to hear. All the old feelings Norma had felt ten years ago, which had been buried under the cover story of her affair, were now surfacing. Not only were the same terrors returning, but also the weight gain. She began compulsively to overeat once again, just as she had when her daughters left and her mother died. The wounds that Norma had sustained as a child were being laid bare once again.

The affair had been about escape from the very emotions Norma was now feeling. She had avoided her inner pain in an affair that served to make her feel better, even look better. On the surface, that sounds good—cover stories always do. But it was only a temporary fix. Now she no longer had the fantasy and illusion of a fresh affair to mitigate the pain of impending loss. Norma had used the affair to mask the issues of separation and loss, but now the affair held no power to enchant, offered no place to hide. Norma's affair had lost its power to conceal real issues. Norma would have to deal with what she had always feared and avoided. She would have to face her feelings. She would have to confront her terrors.

There is no painless way to heal ourselves. It's always a mistake to try to avoid this experience of pain. We try to go over or under and take the painless route, but there is none. Often we cannot see the way, or only in hindsight. None of us can assume the mantle of parenthood without inheriting the leave-taking that must accompany it. It's not easy to let go. We so want to hold fast. Finally, Norma would have to keep her date with destiny and go through her private tunnel. My thoughts, as yet, remained unspoken:

Can you see how you fled for your life into motherhood?
Can you see how you have sought refuge in the affair?
Can you see that there is no refuge, only risk?
Can you see that the only safety we have is within?
Can you see what we have to do here?
Can you see that I will have to help you let go?

Norma had never faced the fact that her inner life was not being sustained in any satisfying way in her marriage or as an individual. Did she want to work on that? This sense of inadequacy was heightened by the fact that she could lose her grandson. Did she want to face that? She was beginning to face and feel that her special affair, now a well-worn shoe, was changing and slowly fading into a friendship, not a romantic dream come true. Was she going to continue with that? Or was Norma going to address the issues in her life and try to rebuild intimacy into her marriage?

As yet there are no hard-and-fast answers. Norma's work of

growing whole began and continues as she faces the loss of a grand-son who is growing into a life that will include less of her mother-ing. Norma's affair ended, but as old friends, they still share a corner of their lives. She is working hard trying to clear the runway of her emotional debris, a valiant warrior bearing scars, hoping finally to soar. Sometimes, that's all any of us, even the best of us, can do.

Chapter Nine

❧❧

Luke and Travis: An Escape from Anxiety

A very popular error, having the courage of one's
convictions: rather it is a matter of having the
courage for an attack upon one's convictions.

—FRIEDRICH NIETZSCHE

❧ Part of sexual pleasure is the soothing it brings. The physical intimacy felt by the infant in the mother's arms as we were physically soothed by being rocked, kissed, and held is carried forward into adulthood by sexual activity. Masturbation as practiced in adolescence is a learning activity as well as a self-soother. This segues quite naturally into the interactive sexual activity of our adult relationships. Sex as a soother is integrated into the many functions sex fulfills.

Sometimes, the self-soothing function of sex predominates to the degree that sex becomes the major way we deal with the stress and anxiety of inner conflicts. It is used like a drug and represents addictive behavior. Often, despite the presence of a primary relationship, multiple partners are continually sought. When sexual activity becomes something that is needed in order to reduce anxiety and is an obsessive-compulsive experience, it functions much the same way as does any substance abuse. Relationships, which are anxiety-producing, are avoided. Sex partners are perceived as necessary to satisfy sexual needs rather than as emotional partners in a more three-dimensional relationship that satisfies other needs as well. Variety becomes a stimulating sex aid needed to help stoke the sexual fire to cover anxiety.

The men illustrated in the two case histories here, while dealing with different circumstances, read much like the same person, because both compulsively use sex to deal with the tension, anxiety, and conflict states of their inner worlds. Their inability to be faithful, due to any number of excuses, is the cover story. The inner truth is that they use sex in the same way drugs, food, or alcohol are sometimes abused. These men are sex addicts who rely on sex to mask their inner state of anxiety, confusion, chaos, and despair. The problems have never been faced, or solved, because they have not been allowed to surface through the constant, soothing, druglike balm of sex.

When numerous sexual affairs continue unabated in conjunction with another seemingly primary relationship, sex as a form of addictive behavior needs to be faced. The resolution of sex addiction requires the same treatment program as that of drugs or alcohol. Twelve-step programs have been highly successful. Therapy and support groups are helpful, indeed even necessary, but the primary focus is on abstinence and the hard work of continuing that abstinence. Oftentimes therapy brings about the willingness to initiate a program of abstinence because, as with all change, people must be ready to admit to their behavior and actively want to address it.

✍ *Luke*

Luke blew into treatment like a storm. A bristling hostility surrounded his body. He was in his midforties, his hair graying, but something about his manner made him appear decades younger. He reminded me of a fidgety adolescent. Perhaps it was the wad of gum he constantly chewed or the fact he couldn't sit completely still. One foot silently tapped the air, keeping time to a beat of his own. He kept glancing at his watch, as if trying to get through the hour when, at last, he would be set free.

Luke felt he was under a tremendous amount of stress despite a relatively easy, secure job and no real family obligations. Still, he was easily overwhelmed and very brittle. He was in the midst of a fleeting affair, which was flavored with visits to prostitutes, and another impending divorce. Technically his second, but really his third. Each of the marriages had lasted barely a year. The recurring theme that had prompted him to seek my help revolved around his soon-to-be-ex-wife, Gloria. Luke wanted my advice about how to handle her. He wanted to give therapy a quick look-see. Could therapy offer him something that would help him keep "his ex" (as he referred to his current wife) off his back? The help he hoped I could give him was designed toward emotional freedom to pursue what made him feel good: sex. He wanted out of the jungle of relationships. He even wanted to get out of therapy before it really began.

Relationships of any sort were stressful to Luke. He had no close friends or associates. In his view, sex was enough of an emotional existence. I hesitate to use the word *relationship* in describing his sex life because his sexual activity, begun in his early twenties, consisted mainly of sexual encounters with different women and masturbation. Sexual contacts continued throughout his brief marriages. Variety was an aphrodisiac. Luke couldn't get enough of sex, and for weeks on end it seemed as if he couldn't get enough of describing it to me, as if that, too, were a sexual performance. What he described was sex; what I heard was a plea for approval, and a lot of obsessive-compulsive, anxiety-reducing behavior. He was addicted to sex, unable to become emotionally attached, and dependent upon the kindness of strangers: prostitutes.

The underlying theme of resentment toward his family came forth loud and clear. Luke was seething. His history described a father who was withdrawn, generally trying to steer clear of his wife's wrath. Luke's mother, a lawyer, was the machine behind the medical clinics that carried his father's name. She was a smothering, judgmental, emasculating woman who was never interested in Luke as a person and wanted only a flattering reflection of her son.

Luke's mother had high aspirations for him, and she kept him on a tight leash, but he never lived up to her expectations. Luke felt he was a serious disappointment to her. He failed to enter either law or medicine and so had been given a job managing one of the less important medical clinics. He felt owned by his dependency on the family business, and his independence had been stifled. He believed that his mother hemmed him in, manipulated him, and he suffered from a constant state of tension over his inability to perform well enough for her approval. Sex calmed him down and made him feel good about himself. He had learned early on, in an adolescent frenzy of sexual activity where he masturbated several times a day, that sex made him feel good.

Masturbation calmed the emotional frenzy within. After adolescence, Luke's self-soothing segued into sexual contacts that functioned as the masturbation had. If a girl was particularly pleasing,

Luke would continue to see her for weeks. He never grew emotionally involved because he wasn't able to be close. As a young man, Luke's sexual contacts were easily obtainable, but they became more complicated when casual sex fell out of favor. Health concerns became an issue for women, and he found ready and willing females in short supply. In an early drunken spree, he woke up to find himself married and quickly had the marriage annulled.

Luke's mothering experience left him with severe difficulty in attachment. He avoided the danger that women represented by obtaining sexual gratification in fleeting affairs instead of in an ongoing relationship. The women in casual sexual affairs were never in a powerful enough position to harm him. Caught between the need for sex as a constant source of anxiety reduction and the need to remain emotionally detached, Luke didn't have much choice in sexual partners. He became dependent upon prostitutes. They were a drug to which he was addicted. Luke was held together by this kind of sexual glue.

Seven years after the annulment, Luke found himself in another marriage and again immediately regretted his decision. That marriage ended quickly in a divorce, and he returned to his pattern of temporary sexual relationships, heavily sprinkled with visits from prostitutes. His present wife, Gloria, was a sexual partner of a different sort. Their sexual liaison lasted for many years, along with his continued visits to prostitutes. Somehow, Gloria gave him a feeling of safety, and he drifted once again into marriage. It may have been, in fact, a spark of good judgment because Gloria seemed sincerely to want to provide a good emotional home for him. The marriage, however, now threatened to put a crimp in his sexual style.

Luke needed help recognizing that he had a profound choice to make. He could continue living his two-dimensional existence in which he used sexual behavior to allay his anxiety, or he could recognize what was taking place on the inside and perhaps give this marriage a chance. Acknowledging that he was a sex addict was crucial. I had the feeling that Gloria would willingly help him in the struggle he would eventually have to undertake in his life if he were to become whole. However, asking Luke to relinquish his sexual freedom was the same as asking an alcoholic to refrain from drinking or a drug abuser to give up drugs. He would have to be powerfully motivated.

What were Luke's choices? He was addicted to sex, but he couldn't continue living with prostitutes forever, could he? Perhaps he would be willing to give his marriage a chance. Maybe we could take the edge off those brittle feelings. Gloria was, as I suspected, sincerely interested in working out her marriage, but could she live with the possibility of Luke's sexual detours?

I also had a choice to make here. Antidepressants seemed a logical addition to therapy. Antidepressants are anti-irritants, helpful in mood disorders and turning down the burner on anger as well as anxiety. With the use of medication, perhaps Luke would remain in treatment and in his marriage—at least until therapy had a chance to have an effect upon him. But I didn't want to broach the subject yet. I encouraged Luke to give treatment a chance. I warned him that it would require a lot of work and I would probably be experienced as another deficient woman in his life.

Would you prefer a man to treat you?
Got someone in mind?
No, but you seem reluctant.
I am, but not because you're a female.
Then let's give it a go.
You've got enough enthusiasm for the two of us.
Yes, I do.

He slowly learned to trust me, and we ultimately began a course of medication that seemed to work in controlling Luke's short fuse. Buoyed by this success and to help him deal with his deep sense of isolation, I gave him a book about a twelve-step program. During the next few weeks, when he failed to respond, I gave him others. It was then that I discovered he had dyslexia and couldn't really read. I hadn't blundered into enough medical miracles and had spilled milk. Mopping up, I apologized for not getting a more accurate picture in a less insensitive way. I apologized and apologized. I could see I had wounded what little pride he had and raised his anxiety about therapy with me in much the same way it was already present in his life. Could Luke trust that I wouldn't wound him again? Here I was, in the same bucket as his mother. Another woman trying to control, change. Couldn't I have just accepted him as he was? Couldn't I at least have known what he needed? Couldn't I, at least, have helped? I remember the session all too well. His jaw clenched, his foot jiggling.

> *I'm leaving for Cabo.*
> *Are you staying long?*
> *The women are to die for.*
> *Can we make a time for another session?*
> *I'll make an appointment as soon as I get back.*

More than a month later, Luke finally called. When he returned, he told me that I hadn't paid attention to him or been considerate of his feelings. He was right, of course. He had made a major developmental leap into agreeing to try therapy on my ground rules. He was vulnerable, and I had failed to take all possibilities into account in order to make the therapy feel safe. The fact that he could tell me these feelings meant more than his continued sexual acting out. His ability to return demonstrated that we were actually building a connection that might one day give him the capacity for a satisfying relationship, even if he couldn't stop his addictive sexual behavior immediately.

We began again, and this time Gloria came to some sessions with him. She was willing to have a trial separation, as she really didn't want to divorce him. Luke, too, was now willing to postpone the divorce. He couldn't promise anything. Although his sexual contacts were diminishing, he still acted out. I couldn't promise anything, either, except that we were making progress. I didn't want Gloria to fool herself. Would they be able to continue on, perhaps even live together, not knowing what the outcome might be? No one knew.

In our sessions, Luke began to see that he had never been considerate of Gloria's feelings, since she had never existed as a person to him. Luke had never taken anyone's needs but his own into account. Now he felt more attachment, not a lot or enough, but more. At least he wouldn't flaunt his escapades and would work on being more emotionally present in a relationship with her and protect her from his behavior. Perhaps someday he would commit to a program of abstinence. For now, he would continue to try to grow whole. And in my book, *try* is a nonfailure word.

Travis

Travis wore a halo of a different sort. He, too, was a sex addict but more on the angelic order. Despite the wings, however, Travis was a blight on fidelity. He was a well-known country western star who sang his way into my office. He had thousands of fans, and clearly he was determined that I would be one of them. He was charismatic, but it masked a deep sense of anxiety about his adequacy as a person and, more, as a performing artist. He toured regularly, and while he didn't use drugs, sex had become the drug he relied on to combat anxiety about his self-worth. Availing himself of sexual favors made him feel special, unique, and wonderful, and allowed him to believe in himself enough to perform. Each sexual affair was a bulwark against the constant anxiety and crippling stage fright he felt on his concert tours.

Travis had an abundance of physical charm. He was a grown man with the appeal of a little boy. The combination was like catnip to the ladies. When he was on tour, he was sexually swamped by a great many adoring females. Women found him irresistible; they lavished him with attention and affection, and he graciously returned the compliments. He always found time to take a lady to lunch. He was always fair. Going in he would tell them it wasn't going anywhere. Going in he would tell them he was a family man. Going in he would kiss them good-bye.

Travis came by his way with the ladies quite honestly. He had been well tutored. He had descended from a long line of lotharios, all famous in their day, all of whom suffered from the same overabundance of charm. His grandfather, father, and uncles all had the same affliction of being besieged by women. Indeed, it was with more than a touch of pride that his grandmother regaled Travis with the plight of the devilishly handsome men of the family. Those poor wretches. Women swarmed all over them, like bees on honey. His mother, grandmother, sisters, and a plentitude of aunts clucked the same chorus. It was a legacy. Who could fault Travis for believing in his destiny? It was a myth he carried with him all the way into my office. It provided a cover story for his sexual addiction and a method of dealing with his inner anxieties.

What prompted Travis to beat a path to my door was his wife Loretta's change of heart about the family myth and his career. Financial success meant that it was no longer necessary for him to be on the road to such an extent, and she wanted him to stop touring and stay at home to be more a part of the family. His career required performing in concert, and for Travis, going from one concert to another had been like a political tour in an election year where he hoped to be voted most wonderful and most loved. If a woman indulged him, he felt sunny. If she refused, he sulked and brooded like a child, taking the lost sexualized contact as lack of approval, an indictment that he was worthless, and his stage fright would soar.

Despite his financial stability and the lessened need to tour, Travis was now in a panic. He felt he was between a rock and a hard place. He worried that without going on the road—and all that it meant—he would never be able to write another song, or perform, and that he would lose his identity. He needed his home to be safe in order for his identity to exist. His loneliness and fears were elo-quently expressed in his music, and his anxieties about perfor-mance were assuaged by the sexual adulation and indulgence that made him feel irresistible. He didn't want to give up *anything*. What do you do when women flock? When a sexual embrace with a new woman lends wings? How do you retain that feeling? Better yet, how do you willingly give that up? How do you stop wanting that?

As a child, he was protected by the safety that his mother and his grandmother offered. In adulthood, his wife provided a haven. During the nearly fifteen years of their marriage, Loretta had turned a blind eye and deaf ear. She had essentially sung the same song as his female relatives, but now her feelings had changed. In despair, Travis brought her to a session, thinking I might convince her to change her tune.

Loretta was not going to change anything. She made it clear that this was strictly something Travis had to resolve alone. She wanted Travis home. She wanted some of the intimacy she had put aside and had partially fulfilled through her children. She no longer wanted to accept the blame for his wandering eye and didn't want to make excuses for him anymore. She wanted a partner in bed to keep her toes warm and body alive and a father home with her children. After all, she was forty-five and had put it off long enough by distracting herself. In my presence, she repeated her ultimatum. If he wanted her, if he wanted to keep his family intact, he had to do something about himself. Get help, get it fast, get cured, or get out.

Travis was genuinely perplexed and clearly at a loss. He was shocked by the turn of events. How could she blame him? Didn't she know it wasn't his fault? He was able to go out and perform nightly, but at great cost. He needed a haven. But his involvement with "the road" felt like his source of energy. His life force. What made him feel good about himself and allowed him to be successful was inextricably entwined in the way he had constructed his life. Communication between Loretta and Travis had failed, and he needed help to understand that while they had colluded in creating a person who was unaccountable for his sexual behavior, it was eventually going to destroy their marriage. Loretta could no longer be part of the unconscious contract they had made, and change was in order.

After it became clear that Loretta was not going to be swayed from her position, the need to maintain the safety of his home base was motive enough for Travis to commit to the idea of therapy. He announced that he would do *anything*—he was willing to be in therapy *forever* if that was what it would take in order for him to keep the marriage intact. Each time he came in, he made a little play of trying out several chairs, earnestly explaining that he wanted to make himself comfortable since he would be staying so long. He promised he would be my best patient *ever*. The naive endeavor, to plant himself in my office and grow like a tree, was endearing, but his anxiety was obvious. I could see how his playfulness masked the deep anxiety about whether he would be able to "perform" in therapy.

He continued sessions eagerly, but his self-image could not stand alone, not for a moment. He needed constant reassurance from me that whatever he said was okay. He was not a lost cause. Yes, I could help. And yes, things could resolve. He felt great guilt. His remorse about his sexual misadventures came in great waves but dissipated in proportion to his wife's forgiveness. He was grateful when she forgave him and eager for any sign of approval.

Travis had no idea that he was addicted to sex. He prided himself on the fact that he didn't use drugs, but he had no concept of his use of sex as a drug, or for that matter how he operated internally. Travis had to work on the parts of himself that were fractured, for he could not feel any ongoing sense of being internally safe or internally creative. All of these aspects of himself seemed to depend on the outside world. The anxiety this generated was abated by the sexual activity. The image of weak, sexually active knights that was passed on to him from generations hid a great deal of shame. Travis did not feel like an irresistible or worthy man. Shame was something Travis would have to let go of.

Just as Luke, our other sex addict, had to employ all of his being in order to recover through a twelve-step program, so too would Travis have to mobilize all that he could in order to change his behavior. To change, one must take action, often an action that one has never experienced before. It is painful when you don't know where you're going and you feel as though your world will end if you change anything. The idea that I believed in a different way for him to feel good about himself, and not suffer from such crippling anxiety at each performance, was a beacon of light that gave him hope.

In my job to shine some light into the darkness, and in my own customary unsubtle manner, one day I simply announced he was a sex addict. Travis looked as if something had hit him in the head, which of course is exactly what had happened. I then more gently went on to explain that in order to be creative without such crippling anxiety, and to keep his marriage intact, he had to admit to certain truths about himself: He used sex to allay anxiety, like an addiction.

He thought about that for a long moment, rubbing his chin, then agreed. Like a compliant child, he dutifully repeated the phrase, then asked me what came next.

Then you change.
Change?
Like a writer learning to write without a cigarette.
That's all?
That's all.
How long does that take?
You do it one day at a time.

We would deal with how hard forever was later. Travis's spirits were buoyed by what he thought was this easy turn of events. He began to feel more optimistic, a bit beguiled by the prospect of changing, relieved that his wife had been delighted, although I knew she was delighted because I was playing hardball. He seemed reassured that he was on the right track, that he had a way to keep his life from falling apart. In the ensuing sessions, Travis wanted me to repeat the program and tell him again and again what he was going to have to do. Soon he caught on that it wasn't as simple as it sounded. He was going to have to give up the sexual behavior. He was going to have to give up what made him feel irresistible and soothed his anxiety about his talent. How would he feel then? It wasn't going to be so easy after all.

But I may never stop flirting.
Maybe never.
Then what?
Give up having sex with the lady you're flirting with is what.
Just like that?
Just like that.
So I just stop cold turkey?
You just stop. Cold turkey.
Like I'm an alcoholic?
Like an alcoholic.

He wasn't going to stop feeling the anxiety, but in time he would learn to do without the actual sexual activity. The experience of new behavior combined with therapy would help. He didn't even have to stop *liking* the girls. Just the *doing* part. They could still adore him. But he would have to take adulation on faith and the psychology in small doses. He was a talented performer and would eventually be able to recognize that source within himself.

Travis's initial good cheer at the prospect of change became laced with anxiety when it began to sink in that change would be long and hard. With his sincere desire to maintain an intact home life, and my beacon in front of him, he was fortified enough to begin.

So, when do I start?
Right here. Right now.
First, can I take you to lunch?
Not if you want to feel irresistible.

He grinned, easing himself into the banter, already back at flirting with me, feeling good about himself. There was hope. And with it, we would proceed. One day at a time.

Chapter Ten

❦❦

Shawn: A Substitute for Intimacy

If I, by miracle, can be this live-long minute true
to thee, 'tis all that heaven allows.

—JOHN WILMOT,
EARL OF ROCHESTER

❦ Many times the nurturing experiences of our early lives leave us with a fear of intimacy. We grow into adulthood not really wanting to be too close to our own or anyone else's emotional world. We avoid intimacy, perhaps because we fear abandonment or fear being controlled. We avoid intimacy both consciously and unconsciously, as if we were in danger of losing ourselves. It doesn't matter that this is not possible—it feels real.

Sexual detours in marriage maintain the emotional distance that is usually present with a fear of intimacy. Intimacy provokes fear because it is something over which we feel we have no control, and sex is something we can control. Because sex is such a physically intimate experience, it can easily be confused with intimacy. Sex is often substituted for real intimacy and sought after in order to fulfill this lack of intimacy. When a relationship lacks intimacy, usually both partners uphold the emotional distance, then blame it on each other.

Some hide from intimacy with a true self for so much of their lives that they don't know what emotional intimacy feels like. Sometimes physical intimacy is their closest attempt at approaching emotional intimacy. The only thing that feels familiar is something hidden. The following case history demonstrates how sexual detours and a fear of intimacy can collude with each other and threaten to destroy a marriage. When sexual needs are used as a substitute for intimacy, as a bulwark against intimacy, we may end up seeking an illicit relationship.

It was a long time before I knew the color of Shawn's eyes. They were downcast much of the time, and he had a great deal of trouble looking directly at me. Shawn was in his late thirties, but he seemed far younger and was achingly immature. He was confused and desperately in need of a friend. He was separated from his wife, Anne. Even though he was deeply involved in an affair, he had mixed feelings about divorcing his wife and breaking up the family, which included one young son. Although he denied that the lover had anything to do with the separation, it was clearly a case of the lover or the wife. Shawn didn't seem strong enough to have the option of living alone. He had no interest in being what he called a "bachelor," a word I hadn't heard in twenty years. He had nothing to pinpoint except his own miserable muddle.

The conflict Shawn seemed to be in was one I had often seen before. There was nothing wrong with his wife. And nothing especially better about the lover. At least not enough to justify having an affair that would break up a family in which a young child was involved. Shawn was so conflicted about the issues that he couldn't even quite frame the conflict he was in. He couldn't bring himself to ask his wife for a divorce even while moving out of the house and into the arms of his lover. Yet he could not end the affair and work on the marriage. What did he want with me, I wondered, knowing the answer even as I thought it. He wanted a relief from the emotional pain.

Shawn couldn't frame a concrete statement to me. The same emotional paralysis that inhibited him from finding a solution to his marital conflict was exhibited in his therapy. He couldn't directly ask my opinion, such as should he stay in his marriage or leave for a new life with the lover, nor could he state what his goal was in seeking therapy. He felt quite a bit of self-pity and spoke more about his feelings of confusion than anything else. He seemed to feel that he loved his wife Anne. She was a good person . . . but. But what? He didn't know. She worked hard, loved him and their small son, and was distraught and destroyed at the thought of losing him. She was panicked at the thought of another woman spending time with her child and jealous over the time Shawn spent with his lover. She wanted her family.

Shawn had met Anne in graduate school. Both of them came from small midwestern towns to attend a prestigious graduate school in the city. They met through a common friend who thought they were as alike as two peas in a pod. Shawn was studying to be an engineer and Anne was pursing a teaching credential. They hung out together, weathering the stress of school. Shawn remembered enjoying the common bonds of their similar backgrounds and the happy early years as he and Anne discovered their new city together. Anne, a soft-spoken but strong-minded individual, had a quiet strength about her. Shawn, undemonstrative and uncommunicative, nevertheless felt a bond to Anne. They had a lot in common and moved in together. A year later, when they graduated, they married.

Shawn began to feel edgy about a year into the marriage. They had moved back to the Midwest, and Anne was pregnant. He had been offered a lucrative job that involved quite a bit of responsibility. Shawn found a million reasons not to accept the position and began to work instead in the nonprofit sector as a fund-raiser. Anne, in the late stages of pregnancy, tried to be cautiously supportive. Shawn's parents were horrified. They were incredulous that he could throw away a career. He remembers feeling very angry at their reaction. He denied having any anxiety about performing in the high-powered job that demanded more of him than he felt he could give and found some vague rationale for working part-time. Looking back, he could see how his feelings of inadequacy might have something to do with the current marital situation. After the baby was born, life took on a different emotional tone. For one, Anne was involved with the baby. And two, Shawn had met another woman.

Shawn met his lover at a coffee shop. It was an idle moment, a simple conversation, nothing more. He was attracted to her youth and vibrancy. Her exuberant interest in the campaign he was involved in led to one thing. Then to another. And another. Before he knew it, he was involved in a passionate sexual affair. The sex drew him out of the social and emotional isolation he felt, and, strangely, the secret life he began to lead somehow comforted him. He felt enormous guilt, but the guilt increased his pleasure in the sex. He felt free in a way he had never experienced with Anne. He also felt strong and capable with the other woman while meek and submissive with Anne—even though his wife was not controlling or demanding.

In his treatment sessions, Shawn's physical demeanor spoke volumes. I could see by the hesitation in his voice and the message sent by his sagging shoulders that he felt enormous conflict. Shawn's gaze was fixed out the window as he hunched over and hugged himself, speaking as if under siege. He made excuse after excuse for what he was doing and rationalized his choices and actions with spurts of hostility that rained blame on everyone in his life. He was gracious in his description of his wife's good character and what he professed to think about her. I suspected he was deeply disappointed with himself and unable to face that fact or cope with how he was handling his marriage. I wondered if he was able to be straightforward and honest with himself. I suspected he wasn't with his wife, and he certainly wasn't able to be open with me.

Shawn lamented Anne's inability to be angry at him. He wanted her to be mean and surly. It would be more understandable to leave her if she gave him something to hate. He wanted to escape the responsibility for making what everyone in his family felt was a heinous choice. He needed to blame the state of affairs on Anne. But that was hard to do. Not only did his family love her, but Anne's sorrow and distress made it difficult for him to be angry at her. Arguing certainly would have made leaving the family easier and would at least have given him a position to defend. This way, all he had were the consequences of his own actions. His confusion and ambivalence wrapped around him like a heavy wet blanket.

Shawn's history revealed that he was an indulged and adored only son. He had been a model child, a nonrebellious teenager, and up until his marriage, heir to his parents' hopes and dreams. Shawn was bright. He was a chemist with an advanced degree in chemical engineering, but had chosen to work on fund-raising campaigns for a nonprofit agency. While potential earnings in his field of training were much higher, he sacrificed the income for interaction with people and the ease and comfort his nonpressured job provided. While his parents had been delighted when he married Anne, their consternation at his choice of a career tipped the scales in the other direction. They were not shy about expressing their dismay.

Both of Shawn's parents had been high achievers and had been pleased when Shawn chose to follow in their footsteps by getting an advanced degree. Now, however, Shawn was bitter about their less than joyful reaction when he announced he was choosing work outside of engineering. Listening to him, I had a hunch that they had dragged him up the path of postgraduate education and that he hadn't followed their footsteps willingly at all. I wondered if, for most of his life, Shawn had done a magnificent job at deceiving his parents by never revealing who he really was. If the affair was any indication at all, a good part of him had certainly been buried. Until the affair, that is.

When Shawn chose not to use his degree and then abandoned his wife to take up with another woman, it dropped a bomb into the family dynamics. Shawn's parents' shock and dismay began a merry-go-round of resentment and anger. They were deeply disappointed and wanted him to give his marriage a chance to work out. For his part, Shawn was suffering with his own brew of remorse, bitterness, and hostility. Within a space of a few months, Shawn and his parents weren't speaking to each other. In therapy, Shawn chipped away at his parents' value system, as if needing to excuse his own behavior. I knew that he had disappointed not only his parents but himself as well. Shawn's anger toward his parents was obviously something that he had suppressed for a good deal of time, but it was easier to feel than examining his own sense of inadequacy.

The separation from his wife and son was difficult to bear, but it seemed equally difficult for Shawn to adjust to falling from grace in his parents' eyes. When I asked Shawn if it was hard being a model only child, he shrugged it off as if it wasn't an important element in his present-day conflict about his marriage. He found it difficult to connect his earlier life with his parents to his present life with his wife. I didn't find that difficult at all. In fact, it was all I could do. But then, I was the therapist. Shawn couldn't feel sorrow at giving up the image his parents had of him. He felt anger instead. It was as if he had built an illusion of a person, and the fragmented person who faced him in the mirror now was simply someone whose existence he could not acknowledge.

The woman with whom Shawn was conducting his affair was young and naive, with a great deal less formal education than either Shawn or Anne. She had not completed high school and worked the night shift at a fabricating plant. She was bright, intuitive, and ready to commit herself to Shawn. She wanted a family and displayed enthusiastic tenderness at the idea of being a stepmother to Shawn's son. The trouble, aside from the fact that Shawn didn't want what she wanted, was that what she represented to Shawn had nothing to do with her. She was an escape route for him *away from* something, not necessarily *toward* her. My job was to help Shawn discover what that something was that he was running away from. I had a hunch it was the burden of being a model son. It had left him without a sense of himself and fearful of intimacy.

Shawn's history confirmed the fact that he never truly was able to reveal himself to his parents or to himself. His parents were just too powerful for one small model son to take on. His father was brilliant. A hard act to follow. He wasn't cruel, but he was undemonstrative and often caustic. Shawn's mother glorified

Shawn. Whatever he did she applauded. The result was that Shawn never knew what talents he had in reality. All he had to do was exist as a screen for her idealized image of him. She never saw him for who he really was. *It was as if he didn't exist.* Both his parents had good intentions. Good intentions, however, don't always count. To small children of powerful parents, especially ones with their own agenda, developing a sense of self is difficult. The desire to please overwhelms the fragile self of small children, and in the face of rejection or fear of their true selves, they develop a false sense of who they are. Shawn never knew who he really was.

As for Shawn's problems in his marriage, were they ones that could be fixed? Where were his actions going to take him? Was his affair designed to substitute one family for another? Was that what he really wanted? What exactly would be gained, I wanted to know, by substituting the lover for his wife? The only thing Shawn could stammer out for certain was that his sex life was better with his lover than it currently was with his wife. Not a surprising statement. Certainly sex was a good cover story. As good for Shawn as the countless others on sexual detours before him. We would have to find out what fueled the better sexual relationship on his sexual detour and what was blocking a better sex relationship with his wife. I doubted that sex was the culprit, even if more sexual attraction and better sex were present in the relationship he had with his lover. By all accounts, I knew we were not yet at the crux of his affair.

Not so curiously, Shawn did not want to get into the nitty-gritty of his sexual attraction to his lover versus his attraction to his wife, any more than he wanted to discuss his growing years and the burden that being a model son had placed upon him. I knew it was easier for him to allow the conflict in his life to remain status quo.

He wanted my help in dealing with how that felt to him, but he did not necessarily want to prod his inner life, for fear of drawing blood. He was hoping I could remove his guilt and the pain of his separation from his family without attending to the cause of the problem. I felt like a surgeon who had been asked to forgo surgery and provide painkillers instead. There are no painkillers for emotional wounds.

Shawn's affair meanwhile was heading for a life of its own, one he was not quite prepared to accept. He became increasingly uneasy as his lover began to want more of a relationship. She wanted to be introduced to his parents. She wanted to mend rifts and heal wounds. She wanted to build bridges and plan a future. She wanted what someone who is able to achieve closeness desires: intimacy. She wanted a *relationship*. This put Shawn in the uncomfortable position of recognizing that he did not especially want a *relationship*. Certainly not another one. What had made him feel strong and powerful was now feeling like a burden. One from which he wanted to flee. As soon as his escape route began to propel him toward the intimacy which he had so desperately sought to escape, he wanted to run the other way.

The sexual relationship in Shawn's affair was good, but it didn't take a rocket scientist to point out that it was hardly a fair comparison to make with the sex in his marriage. While his early relationship with Anne had been sexually rewarding, having a small child at home had wreaked havoc. Unless safeguards are introduced into a sexual relationship, it is vulnerable. Couples raising small children need to protect and nurture their sex life as if it were a fragile seedling in danger of being destroyed by a typhoon. Sex needs to be transplanted to vacations, romantic interludes; in other words, sex needs to be enhanced, sheltered, and nourished by special attention designed to nurture sexual needs. Shawn and Anne never talked about their sex life, let alone did anything about it.

Shawn admitted that his affair had given him a way out, but he wasn't sure out of *what*. I noted that at least we were getting somewhere. Shawn was now aware that he needed a way out instead of just better sex. As a way of finding out what he wanted out of, I suggested that we spend some time talking about all the things his parents never knew about him. Simple things that were secrets he kept about himself. Despite his puzzlement at where these kinds of discussions would lead, we began with the late-night pizza hunts of his teenage years.

Shawn divulged that as a teenager, sometimes long after his parents were asleep, he had the habit of driving the streets looking for a pizza parlor. He could have had pizza delivered when they were awake, but that would have meant explaining why he liked the pizza, what was wrong with the gourmet dinner they had prepared for him, and why he hadn't told them that earlier, before they went to the time and trouble of preparing such a great meal for him. In his mind's eye, they were such a formidable pair that it was too much trouble. Having pizza his way was far easier without their knowledge. The emotional price was less. He wasn't even sure if he liked the pizza as much as the fact that the hunt was solitary. It was *his*. His self went in search of pizza; the model son ate the gourmet dinner his parents lavished on him every night.

I knew without asking that his engineering degree was not his idea. As far back as Shawn could remember, his parents had inundated him with educational toys. Science, chemistry, engineering. He couldn't remember playing with anything that wasn't part of some kit designed for older, brighter boys. He continually had to improve himself. He had always felt as if left untutored he wouldn't be good enough. His child's play was working at a game to please his parents. He went to engineering school because his parents felt that it was the best choice for him. He didn't know where else he would have gone or what direction he would have taken if they had less of an opinion.

At first Shawn didn't see that the direction we were following in examining his early life with his parents had anything to do with his having an affair. I had a different agenda because what I saw was a different scenario. I saw a boy working so hard at being a model son that he didn't know who he was. I saw someone who had never been able to say to himself, let alone to his parents, *this is who I am and this is what I want*, for fear of his parents' disapproval. I saw someone who was desperately trying to find himself and feel himself with his affair. I saw someone who was able to experience himself only in a physical sense because he was so emotionally hidden as a human being. I saw a man who couldn't allow himself to be emotionally intimate and who instead was clinging to the intensity of a sexual experience as a life raft defining who he was.

The trouble with the sex in many affairs is that it has to remain illicit in order to stay intense. When the covert nature is taken away and the ordinariness of life is allowed to seep into the equation, the sex changes. When a real relationship begins, the sexual aspect eventually becomes more like an ordinary sexual relationship: that is to say, it has potential for being very good, or not, depending upon how we understand ourselves and what we allow to impact the sexual arena. Shawn's married sex was battered by the emotional force of his escape from intimacy. He and Anne never had a chance to try and improve their relationship or their sex life.

When Shawn went into a sexual relationship outside the boundaries of marriage, he could feel free because he was escaping from the inhibitions intimacy posed. His married relationship to Anne brought too many of his conflicts with his parents to the surface. Issues of transference colored his feelings, and intimacy was something he feared. His illicit relationship, like his pizza hunts, felt like it belonged to him because it wasn't really a shared experience. His lover, who was becoming hungry for a real relationship, intuitively knew that sex was being used as a substitute for intimacy.

Shawn's affair was a cry for help. He needed desperately to have a better sense of himself and get in touch with his inner needs. The false self Shawn had developed for his parents was destroying his marriage. When we carry around a false self invented for our parents' approval, instead of feeling a good sense of ourselves, our emotional and sexual lives suffer. Shawn wanted to escape, but he was running away from the wrong thing. He needed to take a stand and face himself. Fortunately, Shawn felt pain. Pain would motivate him to work. He was in my office. So there was hope.

What I ultimately suggested to Shawn was that he give his marriage a try. A real try. That did not mean moving back in with Anne, at least not yet. It meant taking some emotional space to discover who he really was, where he wanted his life to go, and why. And he needed to do it alone, without a partner in an affair. Along the path of the journey into his inner world, if he wanted to, he could try and see if he could form an intimate relationship with Anne. He ended his affair, willing to take a chance to be alone for the first time in his life and find out who he really was. Eventually Shawn wanted to see if he and Anne could be truly intimate, and they both came to see me.

When Anne and Shawn met in my office for the first time, there was nervous laughter. Both were uncomfortable with the thought of doing something *together*. They had lived fairly parallel lives, and neither of them had ever looked the other in the eye and tried to have an intimate conversation focused on the other. They were both willing to work toward making their relationship last but didn't know how.

> *I think you're both afraid of intimacy.*
> *Both of us?*
> *Both of you.*
> *Intimacy?*
> *Intimacy.*
> *Do you say that to all the couples?*
> *Eventually.*

Having missed out on many of the skills that are required to make a real relationship work, they didn't know what to do. I had doubts as to whether they would be able to do what was required. Each of them, in his or her own way, was afraid of establishing a truly intimate connection. I hoped their dedication to making it work with each other was the cement that would carry them through. First, though, they needed to learn how to relate to each other in an entirely new way. This meant they would have to recognize their own fears and vulnerabilities and then be able to reveal them to a partner who was prepared to be empathic.

> *What do we have to do?*
> *For openers, talk to each other.*
> *We talk a lot.*
> *By talk, I mean listen.*
> *Listen?*
> *Listen.*

By the way they looked at each other I knew that they had a lot to learn about not only themselves and each other but also the business of making relationships work. I didn't know if the word *intimacy* was part of their vocabulary or if the concept of communication as it applies to intimacy was something they understood. If it wasn't, it was going to be.

Over the course of the next year, as Shawn and I dealt with the individual issues of helping find out who Shawn really was, I coached Shawn and Anne in a method of communication that would allow them to travel a more intimate path. It took a lot of educating to get Shawn to understand that talking to Anne about his fears and fantasies, not acting them out, was the only way they could build the kind of intimate ties that last. Shawn felt that the sexual relationship he had formed with his lover gave him some valuable clues about the kind of physical relationship he hoped to build into the marriage. He also knew that sex, separate from emotional intimacy, was simply not going to hold. He ended his affair easily and with no remorse.

The following year was by no means easy for Shawn or Anne. Neither one of them had any experience working on themselves or on a relationship. For both, being in an empathic, nurturing position, which is what intimacy requires, felt dangerous. Both had issues of abandonment and control. Shawn feared being overwhelmed by the needs of the marriage in the same way that his parents had swamped his sense of self. His fragile emerging sense of who he was and what he wanted demanded a great deal of understanding from Anne.

Shawn addressed what his life's work was going to be in a unique manner. He had a child to support and couldn't spend his adult years in an adolescent rebellion against his career training.

A compromise was to earn money as an engineering consultant, which would garner Shawn an adequate lifestyle, yet allow him to function in a voluntary capacity for many nonprofit causes. He worked out a system of economic power and social responsibility that was rewarding and practical.

His relationship with his parents improved as he was able to feel stronger and more functional in his life. He developed a tolerance for who they were. As Shawn grew in experience as a parent, he was able to stop being an angry adolescent with his own parents. Shawn began to accept them for who they really were. They were no longer parents of the little boy who had been so overpowered by them. They were an aging couple. Vulnerable. Well intentioned.

Shawn's sense of self faced obstacles, but ones that he learned to overcome, and eventually he and Anne decided to repeat their wedding vows. Although Shawn had no real intention of being unfaithful, moving back in with Anne felt as if he were stepping off a cliff. He was frightened that he would disappear. He feared he would dwindle down to nothing once again, as he had with his parents as a child. Like many who fear intimacy, Shawn spoke of losing himself as if it were a real possibility. We can no more lose ourselves than lose our skin, but we can become overwhelmed by the emotional danger such feelings engender. Shawn would have to take a leap of faith that his feelings were not facts.

Staying committed and remaining sexually exclusive became goals that Shawn and Anne were determined to achieve. Shawn learned to distinguish fact from fantasy and not allow his fantasies and fears about intimacy to sabotage his connection to Anne. As Shawn began to establish intimate communication, their sex life improved. He and Anne immeasurably improved their marriage by learning to confide and contain their sexual fantasies in and with each other. Intimacy, something Shawn had not thought possible, became a force alive and well in his life.

Chapter Eleven

꘡ ꘡

Neil: In Search of Self-Esteem

So much is a man worth as he esteems himself.

—FRANÇOIS RABELAIS

꘡ No matter how sturdy our sense of self-esteem, we feel good about ourselves by the reflection of approval and validation from others, most importantly the intimate partners in our lives. Getting back a good picture of ourselves is an important function of a healthy relationship. No one wants to see an image that shrivels the soul. None of us wants the person we love to reflect back his or her disappointments in our shortcomings rather than acceptance of our flaws. We all have them. We are all imperfect creatures in one way or another. Good relationships require the ability to accept each other for who we are and not as we want each other to be. Self-esteem is a substance that needs to be replenished.

Self-esteem issues stem from our early nurturing experiences. We all have suffered some degree of mishandling that has left dents and bruises on the formation of our self-image. Even with an as-good-as-it-gets early childhood, it is an ongoing struggle for many of us to maintain a good sense of self-esteem in the challenging world of adulthood. Career pressures and the demands of parenthood can deplete self-esteem reserves. Often, the ravages of low self-esteem have a corrosive effect on our relationships.

In an ideal world, not only will we develop a good self image, but we will choose a marital partner who enhances this sense of ourselves. But we don't live in an ideal world, so often this is not the case. Low self-esteem plagues us in hundreds of different ways, and a sexual detour can beckon with a mistaken reprieve.

Sometimes self-esteem is depleted by the way our partner deals with us. Many of us don't recognize how we transfer all our disappointments and conflicts onto our marital partner and erode his or her self-esteem. When self-esteem plummets, it makes us vulnerable to a sexual detour.

Sometimes unexpected life situations, such as sickness, job reversal, or even financial success, can send the self-esteem elevator plunging down to the basement. As we try to deal with the challenge presented, we may find ourselves diving under the covers of an affair. In yet other cases, no matter how well we interact in a relationship, or what accomplishments we seem to have, our self-esteem is so low that nothing seems to push the up button on that elevator. Nothing except the fantasy and illusion that surround an affair.

In an attempt to elevate self-esteem, some of us look for a temporary illusion of ourselves in a lover's eyes. A large component of what we see is usually our own delusion. What we see reflected back to us in an affair is what we would like to feel we are. Secret lives of an affair become fantasies come to life. There are variations on the theme, but they all pivot off of desirability. Sex, per se, is not as important as the fact that we are found enchanting. Desirable. What we find in the eyes of a lover boosts our low self-esteem.

Whatever the boost, the illusion of a temporary reality cannot sustain self-esteem for long.

Eventually we have to develop a self-esteem strong enough to balance the elevator so that we don't bounce around to a lot of floors. That confidence comes from knowing who we are and accepting ourselves, not in denial of our problems. When our internal self-esteem is balanced, it's easier to avoid the pitfall of an affair. We don't need to rely on illusion to prop up fear of aging, diminishing sexual prowess, competency in the workplace, or a host of other issues when we have a strong and accepting sense of ourselves.

There are many ways the search for self-esteem leads to sexual detours. This case history demonstrates one type of self-esteem issue and how that resulted in the kind of sexual detour that changed the course of this man's life.

Neil came to see me hesitantly, feeling immensely guilty and sad. His guilt stemmed from the fact that he was having an affair. He didn't want to be involved in an affair, but he felt desperate about his life with his wife and he didn't know what to do. He had not told his wife that he was coming to see a therapist and felt it was almost as great a betrayal as his sexual detour. His wife of fifteen years, Amanda, was a beautiful, exciting woman, but she was a mountain he couldn't climb. He didn't see any way around what he felt was a heartbreaking dilemma for him.

Neil met his wife in college. It was his last semester and her first. They began an exclusive relationship almost immediately, and it continued while he attended dental school. Upon her graduation, they married. From the beginning, Neil was attracted to Amanda for what seemed like many good reasons. Her snow-white beauty and appealing vulnerability hid a rapier-sharp wit and agile mind. This seemed to him her crowning glory. They had the same background and the same goals. Or so he thought. And she needed him desperately. He liked the feeling it gave him. He felt strong and powerful. He was smitten and committed.

Within a few short years they had a son. Amanda, although fiercely devoted to her son, did not want another child. Finances were a problem from the very beginning. Neil's solo practice began slowly. Although their finances were strained, they were supported by strong gifts from his family. One year it was a car, another it was a down payment for a house. He stretched the money so that their life appeared to be one of greater solvency than it actually was.

Neil liked being a provider and had mixed feelings when his child began school and his wife went to work. She worked in the entertainment industry and rose quickly to executive levels. She commanded as much in salary as Neil's practice generated. While this took the strain off their finances, Neil missed feeling that he was caring for his family and protecting them against the world. There weren't enough hours in the day for Amanda, whereas Neil's manner of operation in all things was slow and thorough. He had a lackadaisical stride through life that countered her frenetic one. He felt it was a good balance until the balance began to shift in a way that eroded his self-esteem.

In looking back over the long history of his marriage, he was able to see that the first sign of trouble came early in the marriage with the birth of their son. The child was the spitting image of his wife. Neil often felt as if he were an unnecessary appendage, a spectator in his own family. Amanda believed that she and her son were two of a kind, a sacred unit, almost a secret sect. She demonstrated this special affiliation by zealously guarding her time with her child, often excluding Neil. For the first year or two there was hardly even time for sex, as Amanda was encompassed by the needs of her child. Neil felt completely left out.

This feeling intensified as the child grew. Neil could gain no ground with his son. Amanda brooked no interference in her care of the boy and would not tolerate any other opinion. Neil admitted that it was easier to give in than to argue. Early on Neil decided that anything Amanda wanted or acted upon with regard to their son was not something he would take issue with. Her judgment was impeccable. That was part of the problem. She was right so much of the time. The fact that Neil's opinion was not just simply overlooked, but rejected, seemed petty. Amanda's decisions were all in the interests of the child, and after a while Neil left it all to her.

Neil and Amanda's sex life improved only a small bit after the babyhood years. Amanda guarded the gate to their sex life. Neil felt sexually incompetent and controlled. The feeling of being dominated by Amanda extended into every avenue of their lives together. Their lifestyle expanded to include a larger circle of friends, and they entertained more often, but it was all generated and carried out solely by Amanda. She had a knack for knowing how to throw a party and which restaurant to go to. She organized and directed everything they did. Neil went along, allowing her to pave the way, but he felt less and less important. Amanda was the sparkle, and although Neil seemed content to shine in her reflected light, he grew increasingly despondent.

The trouble, of course, with being in reflected light is that there is no inner glow, no source of internal energy. He needed a jump start from his wife to feel good about himself. Neil started out with low self-esteem. He had less drive and energy than his wife and had allowed himself to fall into patterns of behavior with her that generated even more feelings of inadequacy. The self-esteem he did have, instead of being nurtured, was eroded by the nature of their interaction. And the trouble, of course, was that he agreed with her assessment of him, which seemed to sink lower and lower the higher her career rose.

As his son grew toward adolescence, their marriage became more and more dominated by criticism. In escape, Neil became more solitary in his social life. He cultivated a few close buddies and went out with them. They went fishing, took in a few beers, went to ball games.

The effect felt good. He began to feel less and less ashamed of what he wanted out of life. Neil liked having a cocktail or two before dinner and stopped feeling so bad about not working longer hours. He liked having free weekends to indulge his hobby of cooking. He loved going fishing. He enjoyed experiencing life at a leisurely pace. He did not like the frenetic pace and the backbiting and politics of Amanda's career, or her preoccupation with it. Neil had no real way of verbalizing the complexity of his emotions or communicating the growing dissatisfaction he felt in his marriage. One thing was clear to me: The better he felt about himself, the more he recognized that his marriage wasn't good for him.

Neil felt that Amanda was angry at or disappointed in him for not being more talkative at parties, for not being more social, more outgoing, more aggressive or assertive. She wanted him to forge ahead and make new friends, establish new contacts, in short, carry the burden of the ambition she felt. Neil didn't want more friends, at least not ones she chose. Neil didn't have the wish to exhibit more energy in the social part of her world. Amanda's assertiveness and ability to handle any social situation were more than enough for one couple. He enjoyed having a few longtime close friends. Period.

What happened next occurs frequently enough. Neil's secretary, Stacy, did not have the same high metabolism for life as did Amanda. Stacy lived at a slower pace and had a much calmer approach to everything. She did not have a short fuse and hot temper. Her tastes were simpler. She was content with a far less lavish lifestyle. She matched Neil in internal temperature. Most of all, she seemed sincerely to like Neil. She admired his skill, his tact, the gentle way he handled people. She looked up to him, respected his advice. She liked being around him. Even more important, Neil liked the person he felt himself to be when he was with her. She didn't make him feel like a superhero; it was simply okay to be who he was. He was tired of feeling that who and what he was did not measure up to his wife's standards. He liked how he felt around Stacy. He liked it more and more and more. They began an affair.

> *How do you feel when you're with Stacy?*
> *Emotionally relaxed.*
> *That you are accepted for who you are?*
> *Exactly. Amanda can be king of the castle. I just want to be me.*

Neil wanted to treat his marriage with respect and tenaciously hold onto it despite the fact that he was having an affair with his secretary. He still felt smitten with his wife, but he couldn't live with the kind of person she was. He did not want to continue having an affair, but he desperately felt he needed an escape from the way his wife related to him. The conflict was chronic and unrelenting. He needed what Stacy gave him and didn't want to give up the only place where he felt emotionally repaired. He feared he would have to leave his wife. He did not think Amanda would be able to change the way she felt or the way she related to him, even if he were able to reveal how desperately pessimistic he felt about their future together.

After hearing Neil describe his life, it was easy to see the appeal of an affair. No wonder the balm of Neil's affair felt so good. It was emotional freedom. Neil felt as if he lived in a detention home for juveniles. Amanda had him in a constant state of rehabilitation. Change the shirt, the shoes, the tie, the hair, the beard, the tone, the timing. He couldn't just be himself. Until he met someone who liked him just the way he was. The feeling he had about himself with Stacy was a good one. He liked himself more than he did when he was with Amanda.

The way we feel about ourselves is important. We rarely leave a place where we like the way we *are*. To be fair, Neil's affair cannot be blamed on his wife's criticism. The cover story was his wife's criticism and the restorative nature of the affair, but Neil's own lack of self-esteem and inability to assert himself had contributed to creating the war zone from which he now felt he had to be evacuated. Eventually that was the issue Neil would need to address.

Neil needed help from individual psychotherapy to repair and rebuild his self-esteem. He needed to understand and assert the needs that would allow his feelings about himself to rise. Clearly Neil's marriage also needed the help of marital therapy. When a couple is in marital therapy, the marriage becomes the patient. A therapist functions as a translator and referee for a couple in conflict. In the context of couples therapy, Neil would more easily be able to express his feelings, and Amanda could be taught how to relate to Neil in a manner that nurtured his self-esteem instead of destroying it. This was the only way we could see if there was a way the marriage might improve.

First, however, there was the business of the affair. Being an individual therapist makes it easy to maintain confidentiality. Being a couples therapist makes it a bit more problematic. Ethical questions arise when the therapist is privy to some information one spouse doesn't have. Some therapists refuse to treat a couple while an affair is in progress. Others feel this is unrealistic. I find it more ethically comfortable and therapeutically valuable if the partner having the affair is willing to have the issue brought out into the open, because this gives the marriage the best chance to survive. If there is a sincere effort to repair the marriage, I will not let the existence of the affair stand in the way of my help. We do not live in an ideal world and can do only what we can do. Sometimes giving up an affair is asking too much.

I advised Neil not to give in to his hopelessness or his fears about his marriage. Individual therapy would help him, and marital therapy also might hold out hope for his marriage. I suggested that it was time to stop behaving as if he were afraid, even in the presence of his anxiety, and that it was time to take charge of his life. I asked him if he was willing to tell Amanda about the affair, or if he was willing to give up Stacy. He wanted to continue with the individual therapy first, because he needed to get stronger in order to reveal his affair. He knew that Amanda's reaction would be explosive, to say the least.

The situation came to a head sooner than Neil anticipated.

Neil was right about Amanda's reaction. Before he had gathered the strength he needed to confess, Amanda found out about his affair in an extremely hurtful and unfortunate way. It was not unusual for Neil to go out to a bar once in a while. Some nights Neil went out to watch a game with the guys, other nights he took in a movie alone. Amanda saw his car parked in front of the bar. She went in to say hello, and what she saw blew the situation sky high. Neil was there nuzzling Stacy, the secretary. Amanda exploded.

When Neil came for his session after the confrontational meeting with Amanda, he needed sedatives to calm his distress. He looked beaten up, paced incessantly, and was extremely anxious. I feared he would topple over into an agitated depression. There was so much blame and guilt riding on him that he could barely keep his head up. He wanted to hold onto his marriage, if it was possible. He would stop seeing Stacy. He was willing to work on himself. If only Amanda would be willing to come in. He wasn't sure she would. He begged me to call her.

Initially, Amanda refused to come in. She wanted proof that Stacy was out of Neil's life before she did *anything*. Neil was relieved in one sense when she gave him an ultimatum because it meant that perhaps there was a way to keep the marriage from disintegrating. His relief, however, was thin layered, because underneath lay the chronic anxiety about how his marriage felt to him.

As the weeks went by, Amanda did not return my call, but her approach to Neil softened and she showed renewed sexual interest in him. He was cautious about the flavor of their seeming reconciliation and felt little satisfaction in the heightened interest because he felt it was what Amanda wanted from him as evidence that indeed she had won him away from Stacy. It was in this climate of reconciliation between Neil and Amanda, in an attempt to repair the marriage after the explosion brought about by discovery of his affair, that Amanda called requesting to see me.

Chapter Twelve

Amanda: A Source of Power

> Desire attained is not desire, but as the
> cinders of the fire.
>
> —SIR WALTER RALEIGH

Sex has long been used as a means of asserting power. Many men and women for whom sexual detours provide this kind of borrowed strength are sexual athletes, proud of their seductive power and sexual desirability. Sex adopts the nature of conquest and is a bulwark against the feeling of powerlessness. It is used to control, defend, and manipulate. These kinds of sexual affairs have a strong component of aggressiveness. Anger and hostility transform into arousal. We may use sexuality as a lure in achieving a desired effect from another, but this often camouflages an underpinning of hostility.

Many who use sex as a means of power remember constant criticism from aggressive and controlling adults. Many were abused as children in one way or another. As the family black sheep, they usually forged their own identity through rebellion and sexual activity in an eternal adolescence full of stormy, hostile sexual behavior. Those who use sex as a means of power, or look to sexual affairs as a source of power, feel competent, powerful, and alive only in the sexual arena. The sexual realm offers a way to experience emotions they cannot experience in any other way. Strength and independence are felt through their seduction and sexual control in which their partner is rendered vulnerable.

Sexual athletes, for whom affairs are a way of life, are less than heroic at home. Often, there is an unconscious fear of attachment and a foundation of aggression. Such men and women perceive the opposite sex as dangerous and fear being controlled by them. The hostility that underlies the sexual behavior may be present to the degree that they humiliate, overpower, and overwhelm—even punish—with sexuality. Sex is often aggressive and manipulative.

Powerless women can become powerfully seductive. By seducing a man, a woman renders him less powerful and thus, by default, becomes more powerful. An innate dislike and fear of the opposite sex is present in most conquest mentalities. Fear and hostility run through the lives of men and women who use sexuality as a weapon. Women fear being taken over, invaded. Men fear being trapped. The need to be separate and protect the self predominates. I'm in charge. You can't have all of me. Affairs are coldhearted and divorces acrimonious. Derision, anger, blame, and suspicion color the relationships no matter how hearty the sexual connection. Indeed, it is the aggressive component of sexuality that characterizes these kinds of liaisons, as sex becomes a way of controlling and subduing the enemy.

It was into this category that, surprisingly, Neil's wife fit. Amanda wasn't exactly what I had expected. Through Neil's eyes, the portrait I had painted of her was softer. She was every bit as dynamic and beautiful as Neil had described. She glittered, diamond hard. She carried a burden of hostility toward her father specifically and men in general. She acted out her hidden inner feelings of helplessness by combating those feelings with seductive manipulation. I hadn't gotten a sense of this from Neil, but then he didn't know that for most of their married life, Amanda had been involved in one or another affair.

Neil had agreed that Amanda could see me alone before we proceeded with couples therapy. She had insisted on the right to solitary sessions, and Neil readily acquiesced. What often happens with couples is that each, in effect, tries to enlist the therapist as an ally. I suspected that this was part of the agenda, but that didn't matter. Neil's life was an open book and, more important, I wasn't for sale. If Neil and Amanda wanted help with their marriage, I was going to put the responsibility squarely on both of their shoulders.

When I first met with Amanda, I immediately saw the quandary Neil was in. She was beautiful, charming, exciting, and entirely captivating. She was charismatic and seductive. Those weren't the only ingredients, however; she was without a doubt the most unselfconsciously opinionated and controlling person I had ever met. No matter what I said, Amanda had a different opinion. Amanda was very articulate. Her keen intelligence was laced with sharp wit, and she was as quick as any person I had ever met. Although it was easy to like her, I could see why it would be exhausting to deal with her.

During the first few sessions, Amanda revealed her life. She was the only daughter of a wealthy midwestern family. She had met Neil her freshman year in college, the same year that her mother had died. When her mother fell ill during her last year of high school, Amanda felt her world crumble. She was the apple of her mother's eye and felt like a pebble in her father's shoe. As a child she felt pampered and protected by her mother's presence and frightened of her father. He was strict and remote with no affectionate side shown to her. She was picked up every day at school, taken home for a hot lunch, and then returned to school in clean clothes. With the illness of her mother, the thought of leaving home and going away to school terrified her. The thought of her mother dying terrified her even more.

When Amanda met Neil, he not only was a safe harbor but also appeared urbane and knowledgeable. He seemed far older than the boys she had known during high school. He was clearly bowled over by her, and she quickly attached him to her with sexual exclusivity. She felt protected by his presence, and he literally made her first year away from home bearable. With her mother's growing illness, Amanda went home every weekend. Neil accompanied her and functioned as a stalwart presence during what quickly escalated into the worst nightmare of her life. Her mother died on her eighteenth birthday.

Amanda remembers the next three years as a blur. She continued dating Neil exclusively. When he went away to dental school he commuted a great deal in order to see her. Her father soon dispensed with mourning and remarried, in the year after her mother's death, a woman Amanda felt abhorred her. Her stepmother moved into the house and quickly took possession of her mother's life. Amanda watched her father turn over all her mother's possessions to another woman. She remembers to this day the jarring nausea she felt at her father's wedding. The imprint of her grip on Neil's hand lasted for hours.

Amanda married Neil as quickly as she could and cried every day of their honeymoon. She didn't know why. She suspected it was because she was grieving for the life she lost when her mother died and for the fact that it couldn't be replaced by marrying Neil. Not that she didn't try, she added wryly. Finding herself with a baby in a strange city, knowing not a soul, she energetically poured herself into being a mother. By the time her son reached school age she had already exhausted everything there was to do or know about raising one small boy. She recognized that she would have to turn her energy elsewhere.

Amanda found the entertainment industry interesting and exciting; moreover, she found a mentor who would give her a start in the business. Her first employer was an older, powerful man. He no doubt spotted her sharp, quick-witted intelligence in an instant. He wanted her opinion about everything and everyone, something she had at the tip of her silver tongue. He liked her style. He loved her looks. Amanda went to work as his assistant and took to her job like a fish to water.

Amanda's mentor/employer had wealth, prestige, and power. Inevitably, he made sexual advances toward her. Amanda was not distressed at all. The sexual interaction made her feel safe and, more important, powerful. Her mentor was now rendered less powerful than her, because he desired her. It was a win-win situation. She had no emotion at stake. He clearly favored her, something she never felt with her father, a man she had always thought of as very powerful. In contrast, now that she had a more powerful father figure in the man she worked for, her father seemed inadequate and hopelessly pedestrian. As for Neil, he seemed more of a schoolboy every day. Amanda's boss opened the door to a whole new world, and he did so graciously and extravagantly.

One of Amanda's business strengths was making quick deci-

sions and making the right ones. She had a natural ability to criticize
and reject most material as well as an unerring ear and eye. Amanda
literally made a career out of saying no. Her affair with her boss
continued for years. She enjoyed being young, beautiful, and sexually desirable in an industry that revered those commodities. The
added attraction of power that her sexual connection to her boss
gave her bestowed license and freedom. She could go far in this
business; there would be no stopping her.

Nothing did stop Amanda. She soaked up all the trappings of the
entertainment industry as easily as a sponge does water. Perhaps the
approval she was denied by her father gave rise to a powerful ambition, or perhaps the genesis was her distress at her mother's illness.
Energy and ambition crackled about her. She wanted financial independence and all the material possessions that went with it. She
dined daily with some of the most powerful and wealthy players in
the business, spent hours on the phone networking and strategizing.
Blessed with an uncanny memory, she had the details of scripts and
the names of agents, actors, and anyone else who could possibly be
needed at her fingertips and on the tip of her tongue. She rose like a
comet.

Amanda ran her social life with the same drive and determina-
tion as she did her career. The social life filled a great deal of the
personal life. The extravagance of the industry she worked in
segued quite naturally into her life and only served to point up the
inadequacy of Neil's slow-paced dental practice. She entertained
and was entertained. At dinner parties the most powerful man was
usually the target of her scintillating conversation and considerable
charm. The man almost invariably called her the next day. Sometimes this resulted in a brief affair, sometimes in a friend forever.
Either way, Amanda felt successful and powerful. The important

thing was to seduce, to overcome the power with power of her own. And in this manner, Amanda collected friends and stored energy.

As with most things in her married life, Amanda was the force behind whatever got done. Plainly speaking, she was efficient. She managed all their money and paid all the bills. Before she had taken over the task, delinquent notices arrived regularly. She knew early on that Neil didn't have any ambition. Certainly not like she had for herself or for her son. Early in her career she took over Neil's income and managed their finances with all the aplomb of a financier. Neil remained in the background, in what felt to her a dragging influence on the pace and accomplishments of their lives. Neil's own steady ground, holding ordinary conversations in the corners of the parties while Amanda worked the power players, meant little to her.

Amanda grew out of one job and into another. She kept her mentor as a friend and, while occasionally sleeping with him, found a new lover. As she moved up in the industry, she met another powerful and wealthy man, this one closer to her own age. Amanda's lover, somewhat of a celebrity, hinted at marriage. She toyed with the fantasy of marriage to her lover but really felt quite comfortable in her role as "the other woman." Her connection to her husband felt quite important to her. Despite her disappointment at what she felt were realistic shortcomings, there was one overriding fact she couldn't overlook. It was of paramount importance to her. Neil was the only person she knew who had known her mother.

Amanda's second affair continued through the span of her career. He was an old guard of the Hollywood establishment, and the connection made her feel safe. He gave her advice, lavish gifts, a sense of security, and a powerful shot of self-esteem. She enjoyed being connected to someone who was a match for her. She felt she needed a superstar; at least that was her cover story. I had suspected that Amanda wanted someone to carry out her fantasies and wishes in life because she felt so powerless to do so herself, despite that reality was proving the opposite. This suspicion was confirmed when Amanda told me about a trip she had taken.

Amanda came in alone for a session when she returned from a trip to Italy. She was invigorated. She started to tell me about the trip, then suddenly got off the track and told me about her plans to go on a retreat with a self-help group whose efforts centered on enlightenment via discovering the "shadow-self." The participants were asked to bring a costume depicting what they imagined their "shadow-self" to be. At the end of the weeklong seminar, they would reveal the accuracy of their insight, or lack thereof, by donning their costumes.

What Amanda had prepared was a GI Jane ensemble. She had raided a war surplus store and couldn't wait to dress up in the full regalia. She was eager as she spoke, filled with glee, confident she hadn't overlooked one detail. Then just as suddenly as she had begun, she stopped and got back on the track of telling me the story of her trip to Italy. In the retelling, she faltered for a moment on the name of the place she had visited: Umbria. A moment went by as she stopped, transfixed by emotional vision. Then she burst into tears.

Amanda had literally stumbled over a word, across a threshold, through the door into her unconscious. The word that had tripped her and tipped her was Umbria. Shade. Shadow. She connected the word to the concept she had been explaining to me when she got off track, that of the shadow-self. She realized that the friend with whom she had spent those weeks in Umbria was a reflection of her shadow-self. GI Jane as a costume for her shadow-self was not even close. The friend was a victim of multiple sclerosis. Totally dependent. Helpless.

What overwhelmed Amanda was the knowledge that inside herself lived a helpless infant. Terrified. Lost and alone. Filled with fear, yearning to be taken care of, and seeking it through the use of her sexual desirability. The feelings filled her with fear. Fiercely driven and defended against vulnerability, she had built a bulwark against feeling those aspects of herself. Sexuality was her power base. She built herself not from the inside out, but rather precariously from the outside. She armed herself with sexual desirability as one would with a weapon. It had first gotten her Neil, whom she needed, and then she used sexuality to gain the power she needed in her career.

Although this tripping into the unconscious was a moment of emotional awareness and tearful insight, Amanda could not sustain this feeling about herself. I suggested that ongoing individual therapy would help support her as she worked through the feelings, but she would have none of it. She did not want to revisit the issue of feeling helpless except to admit that this was a part of herself she chose to ignore. She emotionally clung to what worked for her, and that was using sex as a way to empower herself and to manipulate her world. The cover story, that she was attracted to powerful men because they were more of a match for her than her husband Neil, was a fantasy that she would continue to employ. We both knew that she wouldn't give up having affairs with powerful men.

The current affair and pattern of trysts continued unbeknownst to Neil. Amanda felt completely in control of her marriage and saw no reason to change her behavior in any way, shape, or form, even when she began to suspect that Neil was having an affair. The last few years Neil had become surly whenever she suggested anything. He seemed to have a thinner skin. He resented any direction from her even though he was dependent upon her for their lifestyle and activities, social and personal. He had taken to going out more evenings when she was away. And the style of their lovemaking had changed. She felt less in control. Amanda felt as if she needed to assuage him by allowing more sexual contact.

It was in this climate that Amanda discovered Neil's affair. She was in a rage. She was angry that she had discovered Neil with another woman and completely discounted her own involvement with other men. She could not forgive the fact that he had lied and was involved with someone else. She was angry at the woman and at Neil. Amanda did not, however, see anything disconcerting or destructive in the way she interacted with Neil. The notion that he was seeking another woman in desperation was tossed out like garbage. What she did feel was that she was entitled to have Neil accept her for who she was even though she had trouble returning the favor. What she seemed most aggressively to want was to reestablish territorial control. She wanted Neil to give up what I knew was the only thing allowing him to stay married to her, his affair.

Epilogue: Amanda and Neil

A condition of Amanda agreeing to marital therapy was confidentiality. She did not want what she revealed to me privately to be brought up in the sessions with Neil. The easiest route, of course, was simply to see someone else, but she had not wanted to see a different therapist. Once again, I gnawed at the bone of revealing confidentialities. How to handle one partner having an affair unbeknownst to the other and still bring an honest effort into the couples sessions? The way I ended up doing this with Neil and Amanda was that in their sessions together, I encouraged Neil to listen to his inner feelings and not allow himself to feel manipulated. I suggested that he examine every decision he made from every angle before he acted on anything. Thus I felt I protected him from what he didn't know.

In their sessions together, the Amanda I had seen alone seemed to disappear and in her place was the woman Neil had met fifteen years earlier. She was tormented and tearful. She hoped they could bring the marriage back to where it was before Neil's affair. Even though Neil reiterated the problems, it was difficult for her to recognize that her marriage to Neil was in trouble. She did not want any particular insight into what was making the marriage such an uncomfortable place for Neil. She was even less interested in her contribution to that state of affairs. She wanted to continue the marriage, but she was perfectly content to continue to be discontentedly in control. We went on like this for several months, Neil's excursion into an affair as a search for self-esteem and Amanda's affairs as a source of power bumping into each other like giant boulders blocking the way to an intimate relationship.

The continuation of the marriage became impossible for Neil. It was almost, as Neil had feared, a foregone conclusion. The ways that each of them had of fulfilling needs was incompatible. He needed something from Amanda that she could not give. Amanda would have had to be able to really address her need for

her own sexual detours and become intimate with her own vulnerabilities in order to attend to Neil's need for an empathic
mate. Neil's need for repair to his sense of himself could not be
accomplished alone. It was a long, hard road, and he felt his marriage hindered any attempt to restore his self-esteem. He would
have continued to stay away from Stacy had Amanda given him a
smidgen of encouragement by attempting to change her behavior
toward him. However, as soon as Amanda felt that Neil was
safely in her corner, she became the same domineering and critical person from whom he had so desperately sought escape. It
was understandable and predictable that Neil would renew his
affair with Stacy in his search for self-esteem.

Eventually Neil and Amanda separated. Amanda stopped therapy. Neil continued therapy and his affair. Amanda had an angry
separation from Neil. I suspect she may have wanted to end the marriage and couldn't really bring herself to give up what Neil represented to her or take any responsibility for the end of her marriage.
She contributed to the end of the marriage not only by her manner of
interaction over the past fifteen years but also by not adapting with
changed behavior. She made it impossible for Neil to stay. It was easier for Amanda to remain angry, frenetic, and critical than to embark
on an inward journey toward change. Neil and Stacy, however, went
on to live a life where they stopped often to smell the roses.

Chapter Thirteen

❦

Lois and Tom:
A Way of Sustaining the Status Quo

There is nothing permanent except change.

—HERACLITUS

Affairs generally divide the unity of marriage and ultimately hasten its end. However, there are always exceptions to the rule, and sometimes an affair helps keep the marriage intact. This is usually seen in long-term marriages where an affair, rather than becoming an escape route, takes a parallel road to the marriage. Sometimes the affair fills in enough of the missing blanks to enable the marriage to continue without conflict—thus keeping the status quo—but does not endanger the marriage. This kind of affair in effect helps keep the marriage going. This works well enough so that, in some instances, the arrangement can sustain the marriage for a very long time, and living a double life becomes an ongoing reality.

In other cultures, dual relationships take on a less dramatic cachet and seem more ordinary than in our culture. In European and Eastern cultures, long-term love affairs that coexist with marriage seem to be more easily accepted and in some cases ignored with a shrug. Some even become an integrated part of family life. Extended relationships with mind-boggling complications require more emotional tolerance than most of us in our culture can muster. I remember one elegant gentleman who lived quite a complicated life, a confederation of relationships replete with all the problems therein. It was, however, contained within the context of *shared lives*. This man was aghast at the concept of divorce and casting out of his life a woman with whom he had begun a family. There was only room to add, not subtract, no matter what the state of his sexual affairs. It requires, of course, a similarly minded spouse.

What happens in our culture is that lifelong affairs are always shocking. In the all-or-nothing-at-all tradition of American romance, there is no room in our hearts for anything less than divorce. But life is not a Broadway musical or a romantic movie, and is much more complicated, as my patients have helped me understand. These kinds of complexities can be seen in a long-term affair that runs alongside a marriage that, for all intents and purposes, is committed and ongoing. Affairs of this nature can occur between two people who are married to others, or where only one of the partners in the affair is married. What matters most is that all parties in the sexual affair are content with the arrangement, because stability is the name of the game.

When some important needs that are not being met in the marriage are fulfilled in the affair, the brunt of the frustrated needs is taken off the back of the marriage and, in effect, this keeps the back of the marriage from breaking. The load of emotional stress is simply less for the marriage to bear because the lover shares the load formerly placed upon the spouse. This is not to imply that these kinds of long-term affairs are a method of solving troubled marriages or dealing with our personal issues. On the contrary, affairs in this context sustain the trouble. Instead of one or both partners taking the medicine that might lead to a cure, the partners live with a permanent disability and the long-term affair is the crutch that supports the handicap.

Ordinarily, the parallel lives of a marriage and an affair are at such crosscurrents that either the marriage or the affair ends. This is acutely and especially true early in marriage, and in marriages where the rearing of young children is taking place. With long-term marriages, especially ones with older children or where extenuating circumstances exist, lifestyles more easily accommodate an altered state. However, in any and all cases, in order for the affair to work as a force in stabilizing the marriage, all the factors in the lives of all the players must stay in sync.

Balance is a key element in maintaining the duality of a long-term marriage and affair. The personal lives of the lovers and those of the people in their respective lives must stay in place and proceed as if joined at the hip. Indeed, stability is so important in these cases that the partners in the affair find themselves making choices so that everything stays exactly the same and nothing changes. Often, the spouse conspires by ignoring what is going on and in that way helps keep the marriage intact. There is little wiggle room for change or life-throwing curves. A precarious balance exists. If one element is changed, no matter how small, it can disrupt the balance and upset the triangle so that everything topples.

One way to achieve balance when leading two separate lives is to split needs into two camps. That means sexual activity almost always becomes confined to the affair. Compartmentalization of needs into two relationships is sometimes a physical necessity and sometimes an emotional one. Usually, when an affair sustains the status quo, sex is one of the vital functions that has already ceased in the marriage, and the affair takes over the sexual role. When sex is not part of the equation with a marital partner, for any number of physical or emotional reasons, it makes life easier for the affair. Emotionally and physically there are fewer complications. Isolating the sexual component of a relationship within the affair, and keeping other emotional components within the marriage, often simply accomplishes a practical purpose of balancing the scales.

Maintaining a marriage while sustaining an affair is a juggling act. Life must be simplified to the number of balls that one can constantly keep in the air. One hitch and they all fall. In this type of arrangement, the affair and marriage turn into that three-legged stool I talked about earlier, which keeps the marriage stable. The trick is to keep something from knocking down one of the legs, or to mix the metaphor, dropping one of the balls.

Whether or not partners in an affair are married to other people, the precarious balance of the triangle makes this arrangement fragile. Because the normal societal and emotional structures are not in place to help stabilize the union, this house of cards can easily fall apart. The simple act of one person having to change jobs can become a jarring complication. When the affair and the marriage proceed, unchanged and at a pace, it is usually because there are remarkably compatible conditions in place, both emotionally and, even more important, in reality. Such an arrangement needs a predictable weather report for fair skies each and every day.

Lois came into my office crying her eyes out because the house of cards that had nurtured and nourished her emotional life for more than fifteen years had collapsed. Her lover's life was changing and so, therefore, was her own. She was overwhelmed by the task of facing her marriage of thirty-seven years without the companionship of her lover to prop her up and saddened by the fact that their affair was over. She did not want to leave her family and build a new life with her lover. What she really wanted was what she had. A double life.

Lois, the middle child of a large family of seven, had married her husband, Leo, only a year after she was out on her own. Her family, unable to afford to send her to college, had furnished her with business school training, and she was already industriously employed when she met Leo. Leo, who was seven years older than Lois, was an established insurance broker. Lois had only a small string of boyfriends behind her, including one ex-fiancé, and was impressed by Leo's maturity and stability. She had no interest in dating. Three months after she met Leo they were engaged, and in another three they were married.

Lois recalled having abundant confidence in her marriage even though she and Leo were different "types." She considered herself fortunate to have found someone as stable as Leo. The man she had almost married was actually a boy, not a man, and he had wings on his heels. Bruised, but not broken, by her first brush with romance, she felt healed by the relationship she formed with Leo, even though she knew there was a primary difference in the angle with which they viewed marriage and in the nature of their personalities.

From the beginning, Lois and Leo had a bit of a different take on life. Lois recognized that she had found an unusual man in Leo, if only in the sense that he was somewhat of a throwback. He had firm beliefs about his role as a husband and father, and he wanted a

wife who would fulfill her role in the family as the woman and not
want to have a career or look to fulfill herself in any other way.
Lois, on the other hand, was not predisposed to Leo's way of seeing
anything. As a middle child, not able to draw attention to herself in
any way other than to disobey, she had defined herself as the family
rebel. She disappeared in the family, except when calling attention
to herself with her misbehavior. The only self she knew was the one
she had found in opposition to something else.

Despite this somewhat basic difference in orientation, Lois
began married life happily enough. She described herself as
delighted to become head of her own household. After so many
years of being a middle nobody, she was now a Mrs. somebody. She
did, however, retain the edge of rebel isolation about her, somewhat
in the same defiant way she had done with her parents. Even though
Leo had a conservative, formal, and exacting preference about
everything from how his shirts were folded to how the bed was
made, Lois went to extreme measures to ensure that everything
was done her way, which is to say in a helter-skelter fashion and
damn the details. She found little reward in compromising with her
husband and did not feel uneasy when he was exasperated with her.
Indeed, in her marriage, she kept an emotional stance that was
familiar to her.

In the early years of their marriage, they fought the same way
any couple fights when married to someone with opposing habits.
Leo began by trying to be the teacher, but Lois remained a delinquent student. Her description of their interaction painted a portrait of a couple destined to go their separate ways, even if
continuing to live together. And that was really all right with Lois.
She didn't mind the lack of intimacy. She characterized it as giving
her the "space" she needed.

With the birth of their first child, Lois soon found herself in—from what I could see from my perspective in the present—a deep postpartum depression. The depression lasted through her second pregnancy, which came within the year. Lois felt that not until the second child was nearly two years old did she emerge from the fugue state of early motherhood. She remembered the first ten years of her marriage as a time when she was in a constant state of pregnancy. Between miscarriages, abortions, and the later arrival of a third child, it was nearly ten years before she emerged from what she termed "the milk years."

By the time the children, two girls and a boy, were of school age, Lois and Leo's sex life had become somewhat inactive. Never a lusty pair, the presence of three children had put a damper on an already restrained and somewhat shy Leo. Despite his adherence to very masculine and gender-specific roles, Leo was uncomfortable in his sexual skin. And Lois, more uninhibited and characteristically less emotionally mature, was unable to see this tender spot. In her usual style, she became resentful instead. She remembers feeling angry at Leo for his lack of enthusiasm and conservative sexual style.

Many of us who place the burden of feeling sexually desirable upon our spouse's initiation and performance in sex become angry when this wish is not fulfilled. A solid sense of sexual desirability enables us to share and help nurture our mate's sexuality to complement our own in a more constructive way than becoming angry or resentful. Lois did not have the emotional strength to help build sexual intimacy with her husband. This sexual isolation combined with her more comfortable emotional stance of keeping Leo the parent in the relationship. Unfortunately, the adult in the relationship is sometimes desexualized because of the unconscious fear of incestuous wishes, and the sexual relationship becomes impoverished.

For Lois and Leo, sexuality was not on their short list of issues to discuss. Problem solving was not their strength, and the issue was tabled indefinitely. As a result, their sex life continued to decline. Lois's need to feel sexually affirmed as well as sexually satisfied smoldered but never set the marriage papers on fire. Except for outbursts of anger from Lois, and cold retaliation by Leo, the emotional climate of Lois as a delinquent adolescent and Leo as the exasperated parent fed the lack of communication in the marriage. Despite what some might call a chasm in the relationship, Lois never had any intention of ending her marriage. She never toyed with the idea of separation, considered a divorce, or ever seriously thought about having a lover.

Did you ever consider seeking treatment?
That would have been seeking a solution. I liked living with the problem.
Because . . .
I found someone who had the same problem, too.

Lois eventually met a man who was to become her lover. She and Tom were members of the same carpool. Not only were they neighbors whose children knew each other, but Lois's husband and Tom's wife were both employees of the same large insurance company. The similarities were too hard to escape. It turned out they lived the exact same life, only not with each other. What began as a carpool with picking up each other's children ended up as a fifteen-year love affair that stabilized both of their marriages.

Tom was a carbon copy of Lois, or so she liked to think. The feeling of having an ally legitimized Lois's relationship with Tom from the very start. Their affair began as most relationships do, with shared confidences. Secrets. Telling each other things they didn't tell their spouses. At first the confidences were nonpersonal. They lived in the same neighborhood with the same problems. They commiserated. They knew the same people. They had the same concerns about their kids' teachers. They attended the soccer games of their kids. Most important, both the spouses were busy and always working.

As the similarities in their lives grew, the confidences mounted. They found themselves pinch hitting for each other, and the conversations at places where they found themselves together stretched longer and longer. Eventually, when Tom suggested they go have some coffee, Lois found it the simplest and easiest thing in the world to do. Unlike the more stilted conversations Lois had with Leo, she found herself jabbering away with Tom. He jabbered back. They were very open about their relationship, calling each other at home and talking freely in front of their spouses. They were acknowledged buddies. Half the time Lois felt that Leo was relieved when Tom dragged her out to a movie.

Predictably, in time their confidences became more personal. They found out that in their marital relationships, they each played the same role: They were the playful ones; their spouses, the more serious, formal "adults." Lois learned that Tom functioned in his marriage much the same way she did in hers. They were each the "wife" in the marriage, and their mates functioned as the "husband." The "wives" were involved in the traditional roles associated with women who stayed home to take care of children, and the "husbands" were career driven.

The term *wife* by no means denigrates or implies passivity. Quite the opposite. Most of the work of maintaining the family falls

to the wife. If there was a vacation, not only did Lois and Tom function as the plotters and planners, but they loaded the car as well.
Whether it was a ship to sail, a trailer to hitch, or a horse to saddle,
both Lois and Tom discovered that it fell to each of them to do
everything for the family. They were not only the chief cooks and
bottle washers who took also out the trash, but each of them carried a large portion of the emotional burden of the family. While
the family breadwinners were often preoccupied and remote, these
two "wives" nurtured the family and saw to it that the family unit
felt like a good place to be.

The curious cross-matching of similarities became a basis for
their friendship. What Lois found endearing about Tom was that
he was her "girlfriend." He was the first househusband she had
ever met, and their friendship blossomed as she found an ally for
the first time, in a man. His emotional style, while much like her
own, needed the structure his wife lent to his life. He had little
interest in a career, and his halfhearted stabs at writing did not
earn enough for his family to live on. He enjoyed his status in the
family as the sensitive artist and, much as Lois did with her husband, relegated the mundane facts of living in the adult world to
his wife.

Lois found Tom engaging both emotionally and physically. The
alliance was heightened by their sexual chemistry. The attunement
only strengthened their bond. Like everything else about her relationship with Tom, this sexual attraction was a similarity Lois seized
upon easily. Rather than become a distressing outcome of an otherwise uncomplicated friendship, it was easily integrated. There was
no angst over it. They bantered about how well matched they were,
but their relationship never became laced with the kind of romantic

passion that would endanger their marriages. There was no pressure or what ifs. Lois felt quite grounded in her marriage, along with its problems, and had no wish or intention of changing that status.

Like Lois, Tom seemed devoted to his wife, even if his marital sexual union seemed cool. Tom felt that his wife never really liked sex. Without actually ever discussing it, each knew that breaking up their families was unthinkable. Tom would never leave the primary parenting responsibilities he had toward his children, nor could Lois imagine taking her children away from their father, shattering the family unit and leaving the safe harbor of her life. The easy bonding and camaraderie Lois shared with Tom helped them form a sexual relationship quite easily, and oil was cast over the troubled waters of each of their marriages.

Over the years, Lois and her lover Tom continued to make decisions about their lives that would ensure the stability of their affair. Lois dissuaded her husband from making any change in his career that might rock the boat. Transfers to another office were avoided. Vacations were planned to coincide with the school year, and both families ended up taking the same amount of time away. The status quo was remarkably easy to keep all through the years, and even increased when the children were away at college. Because both families were so similar in so many ways, this stability was easy to accomplish. They shared financial status and goals, and had similar ways of dealing with their inner lives and marital conflicts. The trouble came when Tom's wife became ill.

In affairs that serve to help maintain the status quo in marriage, everything that happens usually has the implicit if not explicit participation or approval of the spouse, even if it is as seemingly passive

an act as ignoring what is going on. When Tom's wife's mammo-
gram changed, so did their lives. Up until then, sickness, holidays,
and scheduling all presented inconveniences that Lois and Tom
worked around until everything wobbled back to the sameness
upon which they built their affair. When Tom's wife's illness took on
catastrophic proportions, facing the crisis in their lives caused dis-
ruption in Lois's life as well.

A series of costly surgeries and inadequate insurance forced
Tom out of his artistic retirement and into the job market. He
took a teaching position some distance away. His job and the burden of caring for his wife during her illness left less time to be with
Lois. For her part, Lois could only watch the drama onstage in
Tom's life. She could not change or control the events that tran-
spired and could only feel helpless in the grip of the turn fate had
taken. Lois continued to see Tom even after he and his wife moved
to a smaller home an hour away, closer to his work and the medical
center where she was undergoing treatment, but the affair under-
went drastic change.

Had Lois or Tom, either individually or collectively, been
stronger, they might have decided to try and make a life together.
The fragmented pieces of both their personalities were made more
whole by their respective partners, however, and each was reluctant to leave or change anything. Events conspired to make a decision for them.

When change entered their lives, it created an unstable situation that offered much less emotional satisfaction. Lois found it
unrewarding to be an empathic bystander to Tom and his wife's distress. Tom, busy trying to hold his life together, could relate much
less to the now seemingly trivial issues that made up Lois's life.

Eventually change took its toll. The time between meetings lengthened. Days turned into weeks, weeks into months. Each regretted the absence and void that filled their lives yet could not and would not do anything that would change the new state of affairs in which they now found themselves. Clearly, Tom could not leave his wife or any longer be the "girlfriend" Lois had enjoyed. Lois, for her part, did not want to join Tom in his new and tragically altered world.

Lois considered herself fortunate to have a loving husband and stable marriage. They still had a youngster at home, and she did not want to leave Leo. But she mourned the loss of Tom. She wanted to know what to do now. The affair was over. So I ventured into hallowed marital ground. It was time for Lois and Leo to work on their marriage.

Don't you think it's time you gave Leo a turn?
For what?
To be the child.
Is that what you think I've been?
What do you think?

The silence stretched.

So what do I do now?
Make a friend of your husband.
You mean I have to deal with who he is?
No. Accept who he is.
And me?
Become what and who you want to be and share it with him.

You mean it might change him?
No, but it will change you.

More silence.

You mean we could work on being friends?
Something like that.
And that will improve our marriage?
Friends make good marriage partners.

PART THREE

Finale

Chapter Fourteen

The Aftermath

Love is an ideal thing; marriage a real thing.
A confusion of the real with the ideal
never goes unpunished.

—GOETHE

The aftermath of an affair begins with the discovery of betrayal. And while the affair and the marriage may continue for a good deal of time, discovery of an infidelity is the beginning of the end. I have witnessed the lives of many of my patients over the arc of their entire dramas. Life in the wake of an affair brings pain, anguish, and heartbreak, but it punctuates the end of illusion. As tumultuous as it is for both partners, the aftermath is the start of a new beginning. Whether it heralds the end of the affair, the end of the marriage, or the end of both, it can usher in an age of enlightenment, restoration, and rebirth.

The Discovery of an Affair

Whether it takes weeks, months, or years, eventually an affair will be exposed. Some affairs get exposed inadvertently in unusual ways. We read about them, we are told about them, we get diseases from them, we even walk in on them. The most common method of discovery is confession, with confrontation close behind. After the truth is revealed, the laborious job of rebuilding, either with the partner in marriage, the partner in the affair, or alone, needs to be undertaken. In the wake of an affair, we have the opportunity to uncover our personal cover stories and learn to communicate our inner truths. I'm not saying this is easy. There is no painless exit on the route of a sexual detour.

What happens in the wake of an affair basically reflects a desire to preserve the marriage or dissolve it. The beauty of the aftermath is that there are simple answers to complicated situations. One of the two paths available before the affair started is open to both partners again, only this time much more obviously. There is a fork in the road. The third alternative, which was presented by the introduction of a secret lover, is no longer an option. The marriage is now back where it started when it had only two alternatives:

improve the marriage

or

end the marriage

If an affair is not revealed consciously, it will be detected unconsciously. An affair, like a cough, cannot be kept hidden. What keeps us from knowing the truth, no matter how fail-safe the secret, is our own denial. What makes us unconsciously reveal betrayal, no matter how cunning the deceit, is this same denial. Unknowingly, no matter how cleverly we think our tracks have been covered, we leave traces. We may believe that the truth about an affair is buried in cement, but this is simply our own denial, which is an illusion lighter than air that can float away to reveal an affair with one breath of reality.

In whatever method the affair is exposed, the discovery of betrayal is experienced as a catastrophe. An affair sits us down on an emotional roller coaster where we rocket from denial to obsession, rage to sorrow, self-pity to blame. Worst nightmares come true. Long-held assumptions are in doubt. Trust is shattered, and the age of innocence is formally declared dead. The last shred of romantic love is drowned by the flood of knowledge about an affair. We often think of love as a safe harbor, but in truth we are as vulnerable as if in a storm. If we have been betrayed and love has proved to be an unsafe passage, surviving the journey may be the greatest challenge of our lives. *Regardless of which side of an affair we find ourselves on, in the aftermath, we are faced with nothing less than restoration of the self.*

The burden of truth does not rest lightly upon the shoulders of any marriage. The marital union, if not shattered by the disclosure of an affair, undergoes severe stress. For both partners, there is an abundance of fear, terror, and emotional (sometimes even physical) trauma. Inner worlds collide upon the discovery of an affair because problems we sought to deny are brought out into the open. Feelings long buried and forced underground come boiling up. Emotions not only surface, but come armed in defense.

In the aftermath, we face each other with problems not just

magnified, but multiplied. Each partner in the marital union experiences disclosure of an affair differently. A woman well out of the marriage, and a man devastated by loss, have distinctly different experiences about the same event. The resolution of two individual sets of emotions (and perhaps two separate goals) is what we deal with in the aftermath. The likelihood is that whether the truth fountains out in a confession or is squeezed like blood out of a turnip, the effect is devastating.

For those of us on the other end of betrayal, discovery uncovers more than just infidelity. There are painful insights and hard choices. Nancy tearfully recognized the quandary she was in. I had helped her to see Ned for who he was. But who Ned was meant he could continue to have affairs. For the moment, at least until I helped her regain some strength and clearer emotional vision, she desperately wanted to remain married but knew that staying married to the same person who had been sexually unfaithful meant she would be betrayed again. As it turned out, because trust was dead, it was impossible to continue the marriage. Her feelings of hopelessness were eased by her recognition of the part she played in the affair. And while I helped her to see that a marital relationship is something for which two people are responsible and that nothing happens in a vacuum, especially not an affair, it also revealed how incapable her partner was of change. It gave her strength to feel she had control over the future.

THE ROLE OF JEALOUSY IN DISCOVERY

Jealousy plays a major role in the discovery of an affair. It is an archaic emotion and represents a fear of loss. It has its roots in the separation anxiety of infancy. Like a passionate lover, a baby's attachment to his mother is a possessive one. A baby acts as if his mother's body belongs to him. This is so complete and natural that the baby never wants his mother to leave. In fact, in anticipation of this dreaded eventuality, the baby develops an eagle eye. If the mother so much as thinks of leaving, the baby becomes piteously inconsolable. There is no better picture of misery and despair than a baby's face. Unless, of course, it is the face of the bereft, betrayed adult lover.

Many romantics mistakenly define jealousy as proof of love. Jealousy, like territorial response, is a protective instinct and has more to do with that primal fear than with love. The fear of loss is felt as if there cannot be any replacement. The loss of a love object is a threatening feeling fraught with abandonment and rejection. The fear of loss, nourished by low self-esteem, can be easily provoked. Jealousy may inflate a suspected relationship out of proportion. Or not. Good self-esteem guards against jealous overreactions.

Jealousy is like the smoke alarm of the unconscious and usually indicates the presence of something lurking below the surface. If nothing else, jealousy suggests that there is some distance in the marriage. Usually, where there is smoke, there is fire. Smoke may come from ourselves or from the reality of an affair. A suspicious partner may feel pangs of jealousy because he or she has good reason. Usually, most husbands or wives allay reasonable fears. Unreasonable jealousy is something even a faithful marriage partner cannot cure. Conversely, a guilty partner can rarely set at ease an astute partner's suspicion. Guilt often provokes defensiveness and, in turn, increases suspicion.

THE ROLE OF DENIAL

Suspicions about an affair are sometimes hidden under a blanket of denial. Often, even when reality points a finger, we don't want to see. Our senses, however, continue to operate in defiance of our denial. Pieces of evidence are filed away in the unconscious until further notice. Discrepancies, which in retrospect may pop out like a bumper crop of freckles, go unrecognized. Later, we put together pieces of this unconscious puzzle and are surprised we didn't know all along. But, of course, we did.

Our senses are never fooled. Blatant evidence may stare us in the face and we still refuse to notice. Later, we discover what we knew already. We may overhear bits of conversation where the same name comes up one too many times for comfort. Our mate may have a drastic new look. Weight alters dramatically. Workouts at the gym increase. New hairstyles. Sexier new clothes. Even the scent of lotion or perfume may linger. We may sense an emotional difference. Distance and tension stalk a sexual detour like shadows. In these ways, we know without asking, all along.

Gerty had been married for more than twenty years when she came to see me. She painted a portrait of a marriage pockmarked by obvious deceit. The excuses her husband had given her for one kind of behavior or another had as many holes as Swiss cheese. Gerty didn't see that. Instead she saw a curtain that had been drawn over a truth too painful to bear. She hoped, as many of us do, that whatever it was would blow over. Of course, it never does. Most of us are afraid to directly confront the question of a spouse having an affair. Suspicions are hard to live with, but they often are easier to tolerate than the truth. To ask or not to ask. To tell or not to tell haunts sexual detours.

The Opportunity to Take Action

The discovery of an affair ushers in real action. It removes us from the comfortable place of ennui where we don't have to do anything. Discovery of an affair makes something happen. Suddenly, we can no longer deny the truth. An emotional imperative exists to take stock of ourselves for a marriage to redefine itself, or for an affair to become part of a new reality. Uncovering a secret betrayal forces both marriage partners to consider the options, to take a stand, to make a decision. Issues are forced. Change has broken free from the entangling web of an affair and is once again on the march.

What I tell patients who have suffered betrayal, especially the ones on the brink of despair, is that the real hope of resolution lies in the aftermath. I remind them that the only way out of the pain is through resolution. Either with or without the partner, hope lies ahead. With honesty, the future becomes real. The illusory world we have constructed about ourselves or our marriage evaporates like white-hot steam when the lid is lifted off an affair, but the truth is not easy to bear. For ourselves, for our marriage, even for an affair, honesty can feel like a terrible curse. We know too much. Sometimes we may feel unable to bear the burden. There is too much to process, too much to alter. The mountain of truth may seem insurmountable, simply too hard a climb.

Even more daunting than the burden of truth is the reward that honesty holds forth: intimacy. For those of us who have fled in fear from this threat, it is difficult to suddenly embrace it. Both partners in a marriage where infidelity has occurred have colluded to some degree in legitimizing distance. For Jennifer, the aftermath of betrayal forced her to accept some truths about herself that she would rather have avoided. Her husband, Bob, had taken to staying at work later and later, until some nights he didn't come home at all. Jennifer had accepted his explanations more easily than even Bob would have liked. The truth was that Jennifer didn't mind being alone. She enjoyed the perks of Bob's dedication to his career. She found interaction more difficult than being alone. When Bob was home, more often than not Jennifer was involved in a solitary pursuit. She needed emotional distance more than Bob. It was by no means easy for Jennifer, this business of honesty, of facing inner truths. We are all so adept at running away.

HOW TO AVOID TRANSFERENCE AND REGAIN INTIMACY

Under the influence of transference, we run away from the role we have cast upon our partner. The person from whom we run and hide may not be our wife but the grandfather of responsibility wagging his finger at us. We frequently try to outrun the demands of our own adulthood by fleeing from what the partner in our marriage represents. We have no clear picture of who a husband or wife indeed really is unless we penetrate the veil of transference by developing intimacy with our inner selves.

With the discovery of an affair, we can no longer hide from our marriage partner. We are free to leave, but we can no longer hide. When secrets are no longer present, distance disappears. After disclosure of an affair, feelings perilously close to intimacy can exist. Strange as it may seem, *in the aftermath of an affair, marital partners often have a more intimate relationship than they did before.*

An affair suffers from its own baptism by fire once the secret is revealed. Once the cocoon has been punctured and some air is let in, metamorphosis must occur. Something has to change. Change is necessary in order for an affair to transform into a real relationship. An affair must develop the ability to live in truth, breathe reality, and fulfill needs. For a relationship steeped in fantasy and overt lies, the demands of truth can be overwhelming. Marriage, on the other hand, must improve to survive.

Two Methods of Revealing the Truth

When we are suspicious and want to know the truth, instead of creating a forum for discussion, we often set traps and seek to ensnare the enemy. We do this, of course, not because we really want the truth but because, above all, we want to be right. I chide my patients about this universal condition. When we are suspicious, in order to prove our suspicions correct, instead of asking, we assault. This is not the best way to go about dealing with the question of an affair. This question, whether coming from the side of confrontation or confession, should be approached with as much preparation as possible.

CONFRONTATION

The thought of confrontation usually makes our blood run cold. Questions about an affair are ones we are afraid to ask out loud because we dread the answer. This fear buys us exactly what we need: time. Time to think. If we are going to ask, it is imperative that we think first. Confrontation about an affair needs to be carefully thought out. Any negotiation demands rehearsal and preparation in order to achieve emotional control and our emotional comfort zone. We must sift through inner chaos to find a uniquely personal goal for our marriage. This is not to say that we need time to scamper back to hide in some fantasy or wishful thinking, but time to discern a reasonable outcome and path for the future of our marriage.

I tell my patients who want to confront husbands or wives about their suspicions to take enough time to prepare themselves for all the possibilities of what the truth may reveal. Before blurting out questions and levying accusations, they need time to envision all the possible scenarios. They need to go through it in their heads, and with me, before it comes out of their mouths. They need time to figure out what is realistic for them. To figure out what is unacceptable or acceptable. To know how to go about negotiating the future. Then, and only then, after enough soul searching, do I tell them to go ahead. Ask.

Asking for the truth about an affair can be like pouring kerosene on a fire. Often, the one suspected of being on a sexual detour resorts to a defensive, indignant, angry offense. The truth may be denied to the bitter end. The besieged partner may act as if heinous and outrageous accusations have been made.

In another scenario, when confrontation is met by the admission that the accusation is true, the same detonation can occur. In the ensuing explosion, sane human beings are wiped out and only furious animals remain. Like mad dogs we go at each other, shredding what is already torn asunder. Pain, rage, and fear exist in both marital partners, for different reasons and in varying degrees. What seems most important is to gnash each other to bits.

Ask me no questions and I'll tell you no lies. We shouldn't ask if we can't accept the answer. When we ask about infidelity, we must be prepared to deal with infidelity. There is a crucial difference between being able and willing to handle what the truth reveals and simply fishing for an answer to allay the anxiety and dread knotted in the belly of the question. Revelations will be shocking. Hurtful. Painful. Maybe even shameful and humiliating. Problems that have been put on hold will be brought out into the open. Answers will demand action, whether it includes forgiveness and restoration or acceptance and separation. Bear in mind that asking will not bring an affair to an end. It will reveal the problems that need to be dealt with.

Confrontation can be an excuse to shift the blame onto an affair. Affairs can get blamed when, in reality, the marriage is over for another reason. Lorraine badgered her husband, Dennis, who was my patient, with her accusations. She was angry, critical, and suspicious. She went from one accusation to the next, obsessed with her rights. After a particularly heavy round of artillery fire, where she demanded to know whether he was having an affair, Dennis told her the truth. He felt confused and anxious about their marriage. He had sought out his old girlfriend, seeking solace. He couldn't remember if they had sex once or twice. Lorraine went berserk. She was not prepared to understand or offer second chances. She jumped at the chance to righteously end the marriage. The truth is that the affair provided Lorraine with an excuse to end the marriage. Dennis had sought my help precisely because he feared she was going to leave him. And she did.

Rita and Derek presented a totally different picture. They came to me because Rita suspected that something was going on and she wanted to give their marriage the best chance to survive. Rita felt sympathetic to Derek's distress. He seemed miserable, and his angst was a physical presence that seemed to eat away at him. Sex was tense, the distance between them palpable.

Something was going on. Rita was very clear about what she wanted. She wanted to know what was wrong, and no matter what was going on, she wanted to hold onto her marriage. When she confronted Derek, it was in my presence in an empathic manner and with a calm and organized plan she had forged out of an exhaustive inner struggle with her own emotions. Derek confessed to an affair, but Rita was prepared to ask him to stay in marital therapy with her. As it turned out, he did, and in doing so they gave their marriage the best chance to survive. With or without professional help, this is possible. Forgiveness and empathy are not unique to a therapist's office and are found within ourselves.

In the wake of an affair, the storm of emotions makes it difficult to hold onto what we really want. Many marriages are thrown away simply because we don't know how to overcome the challenges presented by infidelity. More marriages are destroyed by the response to betrayal than by the affair itself. Trust can be rebuilt. Wounds do heal. We cannot undo the reality of a sexual detour, but we can shape our future. When faced with the reality of confronting an affair, what we strive for should be grounded in the bedrock of an inner truth as well as an external reality.

How to Confront

Plan when to confront the issue of an affair. Choose the time and place carefully. Asking the question nonchalantly on the way out the door, or just as our mate is dozing off to sleep, is guaranteed not to bring about an answer, but a catastrophe.

Ask calmly.

Listen empathetically, thoughtfully, patiently.

Be prepared to experience disbelief, shock, humilia
tion, rage, self-pity, and blame.

Allow yourself to feel pain, sadness, and loss, as well
as grief.

Rehearse. Practice the scenario as if it were a drama.
It will be.

Do not expect anything to be resolved as yet.

Do not use alcohol or drugs.

Do not use threats.

Do not employ punitive, angry, or damaging words
or deeds.

Do not be a judge or a jury.

Do not wield the sword of righteousness.

Do not take any negative action.

Do not act on your feelings of anger.

CONFESSION

Truth is a strange beast. As slippery as an eel for many. A chimera to
some. Often, especially to those of us who choose a sexual detour,
truth can be elusive. Truth with the trappings of illusion and the fir-
mament of denial attached may feel more acceptable. Before we
unload a confession upon a partner, it is incumbent upon us first
and foremost to discover an unadorned inner truth about ourselves. Unless we are able to see ourselves and accept responsibility
for our actions, confession will only complicate our lives.

Confession is by far the most common way for the truth
about an affair to surface. With confession, secrecy is brought to a
close. Bear in mind that telling may not bring about an easy end

to entanglements, especially if an affair is still in progress. Confession will not cure the problems that helped pave the road to a sexual detour. What confession will do is provide an opportunity to wrestle with real issues and deal with problems in ourselves and in our marriage. Revealing an affair, especially one over and done with, will change the nature of the marriage relationship. However lightly an indiscretion is undertaken, it will be felt more heavily by the betrayed marital partner. Ideally, a confession will reflect a desire to save the marriage and be made in order to bring about that specific goal.

Diana came to me as the result of her husband Harvey's confession about his affair. Harvey had finally decided to tell Diana the truth. Harvey had spent most of their married life involved in affairs, and Diana had spent it hiding from the truth. He was still involved in the affair when Diana came to see me. I was pessimistic about the marriage because she couldn't convince Harvey to come with her. Harvey didn't know if he wanted a divorce or not. He wasn't particularly interested in therapy. He was tired of subterfuge and was really feeling quite sorry for himself. When he told Diana of his affair, he exploded at her reaction. He was resentful of Diana's pain, unwilling to face the consequence of his actions, and reluctant to undertake the hard work of rebuilding a marriage.

I helped Diana understand that he wanted her to fix it. His confession was a bid for Diana to do the work of the marriage for him. Make life easier for him. He wanted someone to alleviate his doubts, fill his emptiness. In short, to be the self he was unable to become.

It didn't take long for me to help Diana face the question she had been avoiding most of her married life. Diana thanked him for sharing and left the marriage. She couldn't make his life work for him. Luckily for Diana, childless, it was easy to leave. For others with more complications and unable to leave, living with Harvey would have been like being slowly sawed in half.

Christy was lucky to have come for help before it was too late. She had allowed herself to be abused not only physically but emotionally as well. When her husband, Kevin, decided to tell her about his affair, what he called a confession turned into an accusation. Kevin couldn't begin to fathom that he had cast Christy into a complicated mother role. Moreover, a mother toward whom he felt great resentment. Like a child, he had run from Christy's (his mother's) control, yet blamed Christy (his mother) for everything in his discontented life. He threw out a hundred and fifty excuses for his behavior. Most of them landed on Christy's broad shoulders, until excuse one hundred fifty-one. That was when Kevin made the unfortunate mistake of using the "you drove me to it" ploy. His assaultive stance dropped the nickel for Christy. Kevin's issues were siphoning off her self-esteem, blame by blame. The answer was clear to me and, fortunately, to Christy as well. Her decision to leave restored a sense of the self that had been eroded.

After nearly twenty years of marriage, Henry and Justine came to see me. For some inexplicable reason, Henry told Justine about an affair that had ended five years earlier. He confessed to an affair that occurred during a turbulent period in their lives. He and a coworker had been lovers. He had been in a midlife crisis, his future at work was clouded, and the affair served as a crutch. The affair ended when his crisis resolved. Henry even went so far as to describe the details to Justine.

It was at this point that Justine and Henry came to see me. Justine was distraught and confused. The confession had no point. Justine couldn't get over it, couldn't get under it. There was nothing that would assuage her hurt, restore her belief system, or put Humpty-Dumpty back together again. Justine confided that she rues the day she asked, recognizing that she was asking for reassurance, not truth. Henry curses himself. Not for the affair. For telling. For wanting absolution. This couple did not need my help beyond a few sessions of commiseration and helpful hints. Time and their own long-established empathic union would do the rest.

Goal of Confession

We need to search for truth before we confess, both in the interest of preserving a marriage or ending one. Endings need to be under-taken with as clear a view as beginnings. In order to do this, we must turn our attention, sometimes uncomfortably so, to an inner self we have long avoided and see what truths are reflected in the cover story of an affair. What were we *really* looking for? What truths have we discovered? What truth is being reflected by a wish to confess? In the final analysis, what we confess to should reflect what we want, for we certainly will get more of it than we bar-gained for.

There is no reason to believe that denial, which has played such a prominent role in the architecture of the sexual detour, will dissipate with the wish to confess. When a decision to tell the truth is reached, we must assume that denial continues to grease our psychological operations. It is imperative to take a second look at where denial may camouflage the real reasons for wishing to disclose an affair. A wish to confess an affair may be due to guilt, or a need to seek forgiveness and gain approval, or a need to end subterfuge—or it may simply be a way of getting rid of a burden. But to what end? We must assess the practicality and purpose of confession. Sometimes the most positive action we can take in the wake of an affair is to shoulder what is past alone.

Confession works best when an affair is over. It's plain and simple. The most constructive reason for confessing is to reinvest in the marriage in a committed, restorative way. When we confess to an affair, the burden is upon us to make an effort toward emotional repair of the damage that betrayal has inflicted. The degree of this effort should not depend on how much we want to continue the marriage. This burden falls upon the marital escape artist, and it is not always successfully undertaken. The perilous job of dealing with the fallout is shouldered by the one least able to do so. It's hazardous to assume that revealing an affair is not going to require attending to our partner's needs, no matter what course we want the marriage to take.

Confessing to a sexual detour should include compassion, because presumably a person about whom we care or cared in the past has been hurt. It is our responsibility to display sensitivity and tenderness. To be kind. Being kind does not mean we capitulate to demands or suffer abuse. It simply means being a friend. Being kind does not mean we have to pay with our lives or be responsible for another person's life. We do not have to give up ourselves in order to care for another's pain. Very simply, we should take responsibility for our actions, without displacing it onto blame, or causing unnecessary wounds. Do not make a confession without displaying empathy or offering some solace.

For those coming off the path of a sexual detour, confession may be a relief. Often a sexual detour is experienced as if the affair were a hole we tripped into and needed a hand out of. *Embroiled* is a word often used. The truth is that sometimes sex still just happens. And sometimes one thing does lead to another. And before we know it, we're in deeper than we want to be or intended to be. When this is the case, and when the marital partner is forgiving, confession can be a light in the window, leading the way home.

How to Confess

It is imperative to have a specific goal. We should not confess in order to relieve tension, or because we expect our mate to offer a solution. We should not confess in order to displace the responsibility of having to make a decision and force our spouse to make one for us.

If the goal is to save the marriage, that objective must be stated first, foremost, and repeatedly. The marital partner needs to be aware of our love and intentions. Problems can be addressed later. Not while confessing.

If our goal is to end the marriage, or we are not sure where the marriage is headed, we must be kind and patient. Confession in this instance can be used as a springboard for a recovery. Over time, the future of the marital relationship can be addressed as we decide our priorities.

Keep the truth simple. Speak calmly. After saying what needs to be said, be available to empathetically hear a response. Empathy means stepping outside of ourselves and walking in someone else's shoes. Above all, recognize that:

> Confessing to an affair is not blaming the other person.
> Confessing to an affair is not telling the other person
> what is wrong with him or her.

Plan when to confess an affair after you've come up with a good reason why you should confess. Choose an appropriate place, where you will be able to speak uninterruptedly, without pressure of time or hindrance of emotional availability.

> Recognize the legitimacy of your spouse's injured feelings.
>
> Empathize with your spouse's pain, fear, and sorrow.
>
> Display tolerance of his or her reaction.
>
> Listen patiently.
>
> Help your spouse understand what happened.
>
> Behave like a friend.
>
> Accept responsibility for your actions and choices.
>
> Ask for forgiveness for the pain inflicted.

> Do not use alcohol or drugs.
>
> Do not talk about your lover.
>
> Do not under any conditions become defensive or accusatory.
>
> Do not reveal sexual details.
>
> Do not criticize your spouse.
>
> Do not blame your spouse.
>
> Do not lie.
>
> Do not frighten or threaten your spouse.
>
> Do not defend or justify your actions.

After you have revealed your affair, remain focused on your spouse's feelings and reactions. This is no longer about you but about his or her reaction to what you have said. Remember, it was your affair, your spouse's betrayal.

In the aftermath of a confession or confrontation, we can be certain of one thing: *Something will happen*. The end of secrecy brings options to the table. It may mean that the affair will end and the marriage will survive. It may reveal the end of the marriage, or it is entirely possible that both the marriage and the affair will end. Whatever the result, in the aftermath we have the opportunity to become familiar with the key players in our lives. We can finally come face to face with not only the marital partner from whom we desire to escape, but ourselves. Finally and irrevocably, it's about who we really are, what we really want, and why.

Chapter Fifteen

❧.☙

Endings

Perhaps they were right in putting love into books....

Perhaps it could not live anywhere else.

—WILLIAM FAULKNER,

LIGHT IN AUGUST

❧ Endings have existed since the beginning. The oldest divorce document in the world dates from about 1200 B.C. It is written on limestone in hieroglyphs. The ending of a marriage in divorce rarely passes without leaving something behind. Somewhere, somehow, however insignificant the marriage may have been, endings leave their mark.

Endings, in the natural state, mean that something has gone wrong. Perhaps because endings reflect the state of our own mortality, when the life of a relationship ends there is pain and loss and we feel sadness and grief. Emotions run the gamut. For some, the ending of a relationship is a simple gasp. For others, the ordeal is like dying. When this is the case, the feelings are vivid and extreme, holding great consequence. We go through the same stages of grief that Elisabeth Kübler-Ross found in terminally ill patients: denial (disbelief), anger (rage), bargaining (promises), depression (loss and loneliness), and acceptance (believing, understanding).

During my career as a therapist I have witnessed the ending of many marriages. Some endings trailed off into the mist, a barely decipherable whisper of reality causing hardly a ripple, as if what ended had never existed at all. Other endings were surrounded by pomp and circumstance and created a great commotion, as if the existence of what ended warranted the observance of nothing less than a state funeral. The lives of some of my patients have been devastated by explosive endings, which have left their emotional lives as bare, burned, and haunted as a nuclear wasteland. Yet other patients had marriages and divorces where the endings stretch out like a thin filament of silk, growing longer and stronger, seeming to go on forever. And even other endings provided fertile ground for the beginning of another deep, rich emotional life.

Ending a marriage is a more profound event than ending an affair, not just because the marriage is the primary relationship, but also because of the emotional state of marital beginnings. Marriage, unlike an affair, is entered into with lavish hope. Unconscious wishes for reunion and the state of infantile bliss are alive. More than a marriage dies when a couple decides to divorce. Their hopes die, dreams die. Marriage is our investment in a future, while an affair represents an escape from the past. When an affair ends, the end is almost always self-explanatory because of the complex nature of the triangle. When a marriage ends, we mournfully ask why.

Reasons for divorce are not always clearly defined. Certainly when infidelity has occurred, the underlying factors leading to a sexual detour play a prominent role. The triangle can wedge a marriage so far as to crack it wide open. We stumble into a divorce as a consequence; we go too far, and before we know it, we are there.

Other couples fight incessantly and tear themselves apart with no sign of infidelity.

Greg and Priscilla were desperately ill matched. Their differences were so marked they could not find any common ground upon which to meet. They had drifted too far apart, and I could not help them find any way of anchoring themselves to each other. Their only hope was in individual rescue. For them, the only prevailing wind that would carry them to salvation was divorce.

Divorce

The enormous escalation of divorce statistics reflects an alarming trend. Every ten to thirteen seconds someone gets divorced. The families that experience divorce number in the millions. Interestingly, statistics reflect the same duration of marriage today as a century ago. A century ago, single-parent households were commonplace. A century ago, marriage ended at an early stage. A century ago, single parenthood resulted in extreme economic catastrophe. The difference is that today the mechanism that accounts for the same statistics is no longer death but divorce.

People hold different values on fidelity and marriage. People divorce because the shock, anger, and incredulity of betrayal are impossible to deal with; because illusions run high; because we have unfulfilled expectations and no hope of repair. Even in so-called happy marriages, disappointment, unrealistic expectations, and exaggerated demands can leave a marital partner subject to the emotions that push us toward affairs and divorce.

Marriage, when begun with illusion, ends with disillusion. The spell romantic love weaves is one of enchantment. Enchantment and disenchantment are ongoing forces in our lives. The process of belief and disbelief, illusion and disillusion escalates into one of growth. The child's world of fantasy stretches through the long, hard pull of adolescence and on into adulthood. It is difficult to let go of the myths of childhood fairy tales and illusion. Sometimes divorce presents a new illusion and is preferable to working through a marital relationship. Marriage, after all, is a fairy tale born of a day when we believed that:

> *marriage would last forever . . . no matter what.*
> we would be happy forever.
> our partner would fulfill all our needs.
> marriage would bring everlasting comfort and security.
> our partner would never be attracted to anyone else.
> we would never be attracted to anyone else.
> there would be no problems.
> sex would solve all the problems.
> love meant great sex.
> great sex meant love.
> love meant never having to communicate clearly.
> our mate would change.
> we would change.
> things would change.
> *things would never change . . . no matter what.*

We believed that this would all occur without any effort on our part. Divorce is the result of the fracture of these unrealistic expectations, unreasonable ideals, and mythological beliefs as much as anything else.

There are many reasons why a marriage could end, should end; however, divorce should never be promoted as a means of growth. Divorce *can* result in growth, but divorce is a sad court of last resort. Sometimes, instead of undertaking the hard work of change and growth, divorce is easier. All too often we make what feels like the hard choice of divorce, but we do it because it is an easier task than making a marriage work. Like an affair, many divorces are built on fantasy, on wishful thinking, and on the desire to escape. This is especially true when an intensely romantic affair is in progress and steaming forward under the engine of romance. When divorce is connected to ongoing infidelity, the fantasy is always that the future will be better and our problems solved by Joe, or David, or June, or . . . That old devil illusion helps us along.

There are many couples who have divorced and have gone on to lead successful lives with other partners. But most have not. The statistics tell the story. Seventy-three to 90 percent of both men and women suffer a lower standard of living. Women usually suffer more economic distress. Fifty percent of women and 33 percent of men remain angry ten years after divorce. Ten years. A decade of distress.

CHILDREN AND DIVORCE

The statistics for children involved in divorce are even more dismal. Eighty-eight percent of children of divorce see one parent sustain long-term emotional damage. Fifty percent are less successful than intact family counterparts. Fifty percent quit college. More than fifty percent see yet a second or third divorce.

The disintegration of the family, if not nudged along by

divorce, is definitely pushed. When divorce occurs with children involved, the family suffers. Unless extreme measures are employed to mitigate the impact on a child, an intact family dies and it is left to the divorce-shocked child to learn to live with that fact. Parenting is not an easy job and is one for which we are never fully prepared. Divorcing parents, emotionally and financially bankrupt, have a harder time being parents to their children. Often, they need to be parented themselves.

Divorce poses the question of personal fulfillment versus parental responsibility. While parents go off in search of their own destiny and get lost in the sexual jungle of adulthood, a child is left to emotionally wander . . . and wonder . . . alone. It is distressing for children to look after their own childhood while the adults are busy trying to find a life of their own. Not surprisingly, then, there is a significantly higher rate of emotional distress among children of divorce. Surveys reveal that more than twice the number of children from divorced families seek help from mental health professionals. It is a fact that children with divorced parents have more difficulty in attaining the socioeconomic or educational level of their divorced parents.

EMOTIONAL DIVORCE

Divorce ends the legal union, but if we have been significantly married for any length of time, especially when children are involved, divorce rarely cuts the emotional cord. The rhythm that characterized the union is reflected in the music of divorce. People hang on. Especially to anger. To the wish for reconciliation. To the desire for punishment. If we argued in the marriage, we will continue fighting after the divorce. Especially about whose fault it was. Divorce does nothing—I repeat, nothing—to stop the emotional drama from continuing. The beat goes on.

Assuredly there is a place for divorce. Divorce is often a necessary step for some of us who have grown so far beyond our marriage that there can be no reunion. But quite often I see dismal results, chancy futures, and more complicated lives. The future, while different, is not necessarily better. In divorce, regret becomes a sad companion traveling with us in a hauntingly familiar way.

Divorce is disorienting. Divorces, like deaths, major illnesses, and similar dramatic changes, remove us from the context in which we have identified ourselves. We are separated from a familiar place in our emotional and social context. We lose a familiar and identifying trademark when we divorce. We are not quite sure who we are anymore. Without moorings we feel confused, lost.

I could see this quite clearly and immediately with a patient referred to me because of her problem dealing with her divorce. Paula was without a context. Her problem was obvious in the message she left on my exchange when requesting to see me. The message ended with her married name as Mrs. John Miller and left no doubt as to where I would have to begin. Together we would have to discover where Paula was, the woman who had been so badly hurt and buried within the context of her marriage.

When we are no longer a wife, or husband, we lose a piece of our inner landscape. Who we are and how we think about ourselves are very much connected to being someone's wife or husband. And it is this fabric of our lives, when ripped apart by divorce, that needs to be repaired and be rewoven into a new context. When we work through the anger and ambivalence surrounding divorce, we are more likely to be *divorced*. Until then, the question *Should I have . . .* lurks.

Abuse and Divorce

I can say with certainty that relationships that are physically or emotionally abusive should end. *Immediately*. When the sense we have of ourselves is being attacked by an emotionally abusive spouse who is either unable or unwilling to love, we should end the relationship or seek help in order to do so. It goes without saying that if the marriage is punitive, a threat to children, or in any way damaging to our well-being, we need to get out and get out fast.

There should be a very distinct line between emotional or physical abuse at the hands of another and the often hard work involved in maintaining a marital relationship. A marriage, hall-marked by fears and tears, filled with angry outbursts of physical abuse, is not to be confused with the more ordinary conflict of marriage. Weekend seminars where we learn how to communicate are a far different story from weekends spent hiding out from a raging drunk or an angry, drug-abusing spouse. The lines should never blur. We should never confuse abuse with anything else.

Gender Differences

Men appear to suffer fewer emotional consequences, but that is likely to be only in appearance. Contrary to widespread belief, statistics indicate that divorce causes more emotional upheaval for men. This belief is supported by the fact that women usually initiate divorce proceedings. They therefore process the emotional knowledge a bit sooner. Men are less likely to have close friends and less likely to seek counseling. They usually lose their house, their neighborhood, and most of the time with their kids. They frequently increase their workload to support two households and to escape from the emotional stress of divorce.

Women have more trouble starting new relationships than divorced men. Women suffer much greater economic strain in divorce. Generally speaking, an average woman's standard of living declines more than 30 percent upon divorce. Unless a woman has initiated the divorce, she is less likely to make peace with the outcome. Most women rid themselves of their marriage in order to make a statement about what was never offered to them—intimacy and closeness. Often, the unexpressed anger and hurt are what the divorce is seeking to communicate. Instead, they find themselves having to deal with this anger that leaves them lonely. Women have never had an easy time expressing their real needs and anger because our culture does not regard it as feminine. What a pity.

The Role of an Affair in Divorce

Divorce seldom occurs without an infidelity taking place first, especially in long-term marriages. More than 90 percent of divorces in long-standing marriages involve infidelities at some time during the marriage. More than 50 percent may be involved in a current affair, yet only about 25 percent cite an affair as an actual reason for divorce. Technically, divorces are due to irreconcilable differences. What does that mean in the language of a sexual detour? It means that if we've had an affair, we probably lied, torpedoed the relationship, then blamed it on the husband or wife. The legal term *incompatibility* is another way of saying that maturity, infidelity, and lack of communication ended the marriage.

Despite the negative influence of infidelity on a marriage, affairs do not cause divorce. An affair is the cover story. The underlying issues bring about divorce. Nevertheless, sexual detours complicate marriage and lessen the chance for a marriage to succeed. Emotional alienation is a major reason behind divorce, and affairs intensify emotional distance.

Affairs increase our emotional and physical alienation because they allow us slowly to integrate being separate as our identity instead of being part of a married couple. Intensely romantic affairs, versus lighter sexual affairs, damage the chances for the marriage's success because of the distance that fantasy creates. We are less inclined to seek remedy for the marriage when romance fills our heads. When we invest in the fantasy of a deeply romantic love affair, we have little regard for consequences, and we have difficulty ending the affair. When we do, the endings are painful and often lingering, for we have to give up our illusions. Fantasies die hard.

AFFAIRS AND SEPARATIONS

The lure of continuing an affair may be strong, yet we may be afraid to make a decision to end the marriage, so we ask for a separation. When an affair is still going on and a separation is sought, it usually means we want to continue to see a lover more freely. A separation while an affair is in progress only helps the marriage roll down the primrose path to divorce.

On the other hand, separation, if an affair is no longer in

progress, can be a legitimate way of sorting out feelings, cooling off anger, containing rage. The hope is that being separate will pave the way for constructive change to occur in the marriage. The best outcome of separation is that we begin to understand that we have to let go of our illusions and come to grips with what is real in ourselves and in our lives.

Reasons for the End of an Affair

Affairs usually end because they don't represent well-thought-out choices at the right time or place in our lives. Statistics show that 80 percent of those who divorce during an affair regret the decision, and over 75 percent who marry partners in an affair eventually divorce. The divorce rate and the ratio of infidelity are much higher among marriages to partners in an affair.

The reason for the dismal chance of success in remarriage to partners in an affair lies not only in the primary issues that interfere with intimacy but also in the impoverished selection process. Our method for "choosing" a person with whom we have an affair differs dramatically from how we "choose" a mate. Because we often end up in an affair with someone who was in the right place at the wrong time, the affair usually ends. When it does, it does so for one of three reasons: The third party wants out; the affair dies a natural death; or the affair is sacrificed for the sake of the marriage.

THE THIRD PARTY

Ending an affair is a complicated piece of business. It is simpler, although not less painful, for a third party to end an affair because he or she usually has the pressure of wanting a change in the status of the affair relationship on his or her side. The third party is the person outside the marital union. For example, even if two lovers in an affair are married to other people, individually each is the "third party" to the other's marital relationship. The premise for this is that the marital relationship is always the primary relationship.

When, in effect, the third party gets tired of being the third party, he or she usually ends the relationship because he or she realizes that the lover is not going to end the marriage. He or she is tired of having a secondary role in his or her lover's life. The third party wants to be married to the lover, but perhaps the lover is too ambivalent or reluctant to give up the marriage. This is the most common reason why an affair ends. Someone wants something *more*.

At one point in my practice I had three patients, each ending an affair for different reasons. June was the unmarried third party in an affair. She was starting to get wise to her situation, and I hoped she would do what most people do in an affair when they get smart: end the affair. Getting June to recognize that she was in the least primary position was difficult because she did not want to give up an illusion she desperately wanted to believe—that of being most important to her married lover. Her therapy would have to deliver the painful message of a different reality.

NATURAL DEATH

Hal was ending an affair that exemplified the second most common reason why affairs end. In effect, the affair dies a natural death. This occurs when reality takes a toll. Affairs with a low emotional attachment are usually kept secret and end in their time. This was the case with Hal. His secret lover wanted more than he did and accused him of losing interest. Continuing the affair was extracting an enormous price.

He came to see me for the express purpose of getting support to end his affair. He didn't want to do what his lover urged, which was to take the affair public and confess to his wife. He wanted to do what he felt was a heel's way out. To keep it a secret, end it, and get back to his life. He had lost the zest for the affair. He felt guilty and feared that his lover's accusation reflected a shallow and rotten aspect of his personality.

My job was to show him that being a heel was being human and that if he let his lover down as gently as possible, it was okay to do so. He was entitled to find his way back to the life he wanted to lead. What was not okay was to disappear in an inhumane way without an explanation or a good-bye. At least that was my definition of a heel. Losing interest was not as accurate a description of his feelings about the affair as the fantasy was losing steam. When reality punctures the illusions in an affair, some of the hot air escapes.

When an affair isn't worth what it costs, on an emotional level or in reality, it dies. When exposed to time and reality, most affairs do just that. Of course, the discovery of an affair by a marital partner is a sure way to introduce reality, but that kind of reality carries with it an inherent risk: Knowledge may end the marriage. Usually, exposing the relationship is avoided at all costs because on a sexual detour what we are seeking is escape, not confrontation or confession.

SAVING THE MARRIAGE

This brings us to the third reason an affair ends. Sometimes an affair is sacrificed in order to save the marriage. This is done either at the request of the marriage partner, or voluntarily, "for the sake of the marriage," which usually means children are involved. Family ties are treasured and binding and difficult to sever.

In basically good marriages, there may be enough common sense to end the affair. Affairs occur even in good marriages. Sometimes a glitch in the emotional road trips someone in a good marriage into an affair. It happens. And when it does, the recognition that the marriage is worth saving often runs headlong into the emotional entanglements of the affair. This collision makes ending an affair for this reason the most difficult.

Sacrificing an ongoing passionate affair for the sake of the marriage is by far the hardest decision to reach and to implement because there is so much fantasy and illusion present. Sometimes, the very notion of separation heats up the affair. Any attempt by the star-crossed lovers to end the affair still in full session not only fails, but fuels the drama. Very potent realism is necessary to stop an affair in its tracks for the sake of the marriage.

Giving up an affair in order for a marriage to survive is difficult to go through. Lovers miss each other for months and years. Berta was in the painful process of ending the affair. Step by painful step. She worked in an office where her lover was one of the managing partners. She couldn't face giving up the daily life of her children and, for her, this would have been a reality. Her husband, Jeff, an earnest, hard-working engineer, would have demanded full or equal custody had she continued the affair and left him. Berta also had trouble giving up the fantasy of what life might have to offer as the wife of a more flamboyant lover. The fantasy provided a life she would rather live. The key word being *fantasy*.

Berta's lover had been in a long-term relationship more than once before his marriage and had been in several relationships, even affairs, before he became involved with Berta. Her fears that her lover was an unstable relationship risk were not ill founded, but her other wishes continued to overwhelm her. The affair represented a secret second life to Berta, one she fantasied about greatly. To end the affair meant that Berta would have to give up the fantasy of a new identity. Therapy was crucial in helping Berta end the affair. She went to great lengths to do so. I encouraged her to change jobs, even her neighborhood, so that her lifestyle would keep her away from the lure of continuing her affair, which can be as powerful as any drug.

It is hard to give up an affair while it is in full swing because it means we have to trade escape for problem solving, fantasy and illusion for reality. This is not an even trade. When disillusion has not yet set in and the affair is our drug of choice, it fills unmet needs. The trappings of an affair are usually such that the day-to-day objective reality of marital life doesn't have much of a chance. Giving up an affair to save a marriage may mean renouncing what we yearn for and tackling the job of making life work with what we have. We may do so, but with reluctance. Could've been, would've been, and should've been continue to haunt. Ending an affair means trading in snake oil for some real medicine. No one wants real medicine.

Giving up an affair completely is almost always the only way to save a marriage. Fidelity is a conscious choice. It means taking the long-term view instead of short-term gratification. It is a commitment. There can be no recovery of restoration of the marriage until the affair is over. Honesty and openness, the rebuilding of trust, cannot be partners to an affair. Giving up an affair to save the marriage must be treated as an emergency. In order to do so successfully, the affair must be treated like a drug and given up just as stringently. And in so doing, we will suffer the pangs of withdrawal.

There is only one time to end an affair: sooner rather than later. Often the betrayed spouse knows better than anyone else how necessary permanent separation from the partner in the affair is as a first step to restoring trust. Sometimes families go to extreme measures to assure that this separation is effective. Careers are sacrificed, friendships ended, and schools changed in the interest of ending an affair and preserving a marriage.

Letting Go

Ending an affair is one act. Letting go is another. Sometimes it is harder to let go of something on an emotional level than to end it in reality. Divorce often reflects the fact that the emotional reality is different from the legal one. Whether it is a marriage or an affair, the difficulty in letting go reminds me of a story a patient told me:

> Two priests were traveling through the forest. They came to a river where stood a lovely woman. She asked to be carried across the river. One of the priests willingly picked her up and ferried her across. He put her down on the opposite bank where she gratefully thanked him. Days passed as the priests continued traveling, but one of the priests had grown strangely silent. As they were nearing the end of their journey, the quiet priest confided what had been troubling him. "We are sworn not to touch women, yet you held that woman very close to you when crossing the river." The other priest thought for a moment before he replied, "How strange, I only carried the woman across the river. You are carrying her still."

In grasping the opportunity presented by the crisis of the endings in our lives, and then in letting go, we can prepare for a new start. It is only when we finally let go of the hopes, the dreams, and the anger that we are able to have a beginning. In the book *Transitions,* William Bridges makes the wonderful observation that the sine qua nons of beginnings are endings. It is very true that going through the end of a relationship, we learn it isn't the end at all, simply the beginning of transition.

Chapter Sixteen

❧❧

Beginnings

Things don't change,
but by and by our wishes change.

—MARCEL PROUST

❧ Beginnings, unlike new chapters, rarely happen neatly. Turning over a new leaf is not as easy as turning a page. Rarely do we wake up with the cheery thought of how great it is that we get an opportunity to rise like a phoenix out of the ashes of our lives. No one gives thanks for the chance to embark on a painful journey within. At least not in the beginning.

Beginnings are tricky. We rarely have them firmly in our grasp. Endings leave so many ragged edges that the end of one phase of our lives and the beginning of another blur and flow into each other like watercolors. By definition, beginnings are the end of something—and that end lingers on into the new phase of our life. Between the old and the new, the past and the future, lies an emotionally scarred landscape that to some feels like a valley of despair they cannot cross. To others, a new beginning is a far simpler journey. Whether the bridge is long or short, we usually make the crossing in a state of emotional flux, sometimes without even knowing where we are or what we are doing.

The best way to navigate the space between old and new, past and present, endings and beginnings is simply to allow our feelings to exist. To feel our way through. We must lose ourselves to our particular loss, great or small. We must allow the emotional field to lie fallow. This might mean we don't do much of anything. We are in a state of limbo. This comes quite naturally with the shock of endings. Maybe we stare into space. Or wander aimlessly. Even feel numb. We flounder. We sleep. Or we don't sleep. We work. Or we don't work. We see without seeing. We hear without hearing. We eat without tasting. We feel disconnected from the past and not yet emotionally secure in the present. Thus with the help of a ritualized passage of ordinary routine, without even knowing it, we heal.

I learned the lesson of healing from a friend of mine. I watched her go through several misfortunes, one after another. The death of a parent, her own illness, her husband's affair, and their subsequent divorce. Through it all she kept her routine as intact as possible. She got up each morning, did her daily jog or some physical activity, went to work, kept her appointments, continued the evening schedule, and dropped into bed promptly at nine.

I felt frantic watching her. I hollered that she should crash, weep for a month, scream every night. There should be some change, I ranted, foolish child that I was. I would declare all sorts of hysteria. She looked at me in horror and explained that her routine was like a strand of pearls. Routine was the knot that held each pearl together. She was going from knot to knot so that she could stay intact. The hardest part of all was enduring and going on. Falling apart was easy. The hard work of change had to take place under an emotional scab. Routine held everything together long enough for scabs to form so that she could heal.

We can spend our time in the overlap between endings and beginnings, trying to understand ourselves. This foundation of better knowing our inner needs lends shape to the action of a new beginning as the disintegration of the old becomes reintegrated in a new identity. This "trying to understand" is an activity, but it is an internal one not obvious to the naked eye.

The wake of an affair presents us with a demarcation line between the old and new. With an ending, the past and the future are clearly spelled out for us. We don't have to muddle through years of not knowing what or where we are. In the wake of an affair we become the divorced, the reunited, the remarried, or even the single again. We may be in the external context of a new identity before we emotionally catch up, but at least we know what world we will have to operate in.

Forgiveness

The transition from endings to beginnings takes time. It takes time to recover from having an affair or from the betrayal of one. We need time to go from the end of a marriage to the beginning of a new one. We need time to adjust to being alone. Whether our course is that of rebuilding the marriage, ending the marriage, building a relationship with a new partner, or even living single, the tasks left to us are relatively the same and involve restoring a sense of self-worth. Beginnings start with the forgiveness of ourselves and of others.

Recovery from betrayal, from the end of the affair, and from divorce requires that we let go of anger and resentment, illusion and disappointment. In each case we must take responsibility for our actions, forgive ourselves, and make a new start. The recovery of a marriage after an affair depends upon the restoration and rebuilding of trust. It is crucial. We need to forgive ourselves for being who we are, flawed and imperfect, and we need our partners to forgive us and accept us as well. Anger is corrosive. And anger turned inward becomes depression.

Forgiveness is giving up resentment or the desire to punish. The dictionary characterizes forgiveness as giving up a right and a claim. Forgiveness is something we must ask for in words, consciously and often. It is helpful and healing to ask for it repeatedly. That doesn't mean we apologize forever, but we demonstrate our sincerity by asking instead of expecting. An appeal for forgiveness demonstrates an intention of honesty and our commitment. Marriage has a better chance if we stand united against a common enemy, the enemy being the one outside the marriage. Forgiveness, like trust, doesn't happen overnight or on a weekend. It takes time. The person asking for forgiveness and the one giving it are both responsible for healing.

Forgiveness does not apply only when there is a wish to restore a marriage. Forgiveness plays a crucial part whether we are going to be single or build a relationship with another. Hurt, bitterness, and resentment keep us attached to the past in a way that precludes building the future. We have to forgive ourselves for the role we played in the end of a relationship, however large or small, by recognizing our contribution to the failure of the relationship. We also have to forgive our partner, or we will remain bound to him or her forever. Taking responsibility for our role in an affair does not mean taking the blame. It simply means acknowledging our part, then forgiving ourselves for it and learning from it. When we are able to look inward, accept ourselves, and acknowledge our own mistakes, we can build a better future.

Even when we are hurt and forgiveness is difficult, it is crucial if we want to rebuild a marriage. Can you imagine how hard it would be to restore a marriage if the spouse wouldn't agree to forgive and forget? I constantly reminded Cindy of the roadblocks she was throwing into the path of restoring her marriage. She had the memory of an elephant. She insisted that she forgave, but wouldn't. She couldn't forget one moment of her husband's affair. Even while she swore to me that she forgave him, she rehashed every little crime he had committed. I gently reminded her that forgiveness meant putting something away. As in *forget*. But Cindy could not let go. She drew each action out to be examined, questioned, looked at, and turned over like a moon rock. She insisted that she wasn't passing judgment. Of course I knew her husband couldn't possibly feel forgiven. Her husband's trial was still in active session, and Cindy's verdict was not yet really in.

Forgiving includes reshaping our expectations about the partner in our life. Forgiveness requires that we recognize that a partner cannot fulfill all our needs or do for us what we can or should be doing for ourselves. Our partner cannot function for what it is that we hide from or are afraid to develop in ourselves. When we are too ashamed of ourselves, or feel ashamed by what we perceive has happened to us, we can restore a sense of power and reshape our destiny by forgiving ourselves. This forgiveness allows us to share ourselves more readily. It restores hope and allows us to take constructive action.

Communication

The way people forge a lasting, intimate relationship is a compli-cated piece of work. The word *relationship* reveals a clue as to how we go about it:

Relationship means to reconnect.

A relationship means a coming together again and again of two different individuals, psychically distinct from each other. A relationship isn't forged and forgotten. It must be a constant reenaction.

The burden in marriage of maintaining this relationship, of promoting this ongoing reconnection, falls not to mind reading or romantic union but to communication. The ability to communicate determines the success of a relationship. In marriage, where a rela-tionship is paramount, behavior comes first. The behavior in this case is the way we communicate.

In relationships old or new, this means learning how to com-municate in a way that builds intimacy. This is not done just with a leap of faith, but by putting into action that which we have set as a new priority. We learn a new process in word and by deed. Women are more likely than men to identify intimacy as commu-nication and set this as a priority. Males might groan at a process approach to relating with its rules and guidelines, but they actually love the idea of simple and clear communication. Mostly, they like the fact that learning how to communicate a new way will mean no arguing.

A beginning requires developing the ability to relate differently and to communicate honestly and openly. We can learn how to do this by designating communication as a priority. We need to set aside time to give that priority our individual attention and use the process outlined in the following pages. This needs the commitment and undivided attention of two people. It requires time, energy, willingness, honesty, and enthusiasm. One cannot do it for the other. We are each responsible for bringing about the conditions of our own satisfaction. By setting aside time to talk about specific problems and listen to each other, we allow communication to become an emotionally safe place where we can reveal our feelings and air our differences without damaging the marriage.

Communication is a process that is both verbal and nonverbal. Sexuality, as a primary form of nonverbal communication, is an important part of marriage. However, problems in relationships cannot be addressed nonverbally. They must be addressed verbally in order to be solved.

Nonverbal communication is always present in nuances. The trouble, however, is that when we have a problem in the relationship, nothing can solve the problem except talking. In order to solve problems, we have to learn how to communicate. Our hopes and dreams do not reside in another's eyes but in the way we handle conflict, the way we communicate with each other.

Communication has an added benefit because it not only builds intimacy with another but it also helps us to discover ourselves. One of the most profound ways we can discover ourselves is by talking to our partner in a relationship. In the process of relating that discovery, and in being accepted and understood, we find validation and self-esteem. Therapy relies on this method. When we listen to someone else express himself or herself, we return this feeling. Intimacy in marriage is built on this exchange.

The more we speak to someone who listens, the more we feel understood. Many call the feeling of being *empathetically* understood being loved. Being empathetic means that we step outside of ourselves and try to put ourselves in someone else's shoes. The job of the therapist, to empathetically understand, is something every marriage partner must learn. In therapy, the therapist listens and the patient talks. In relationships, we trade off these jobs. Each partner in a marriage should learn how to function as the therapist for the other so that they are able to solve problems. There is no other way to resolve conflicts.

Problem solving is really about communication. It's the way we not only make a decision about what to do but also how we negotiate our differences and go about having our needs met. Often when we try to solve problems, emotions get stirred up. An argument starts. The fight, no matter what the content, is always about blaming each other. Fundamental issues are not addressed in a constructive way. Bonds and ties are not forged because we do not really listen to each other. We have no way of being intimate.

Relationships are fraught with pitfalls. Marriages are made up of terribly fragile, vulnerable people. Studies on divorce have found that the likelihood of divorce can be predicted by how couples handle their personal conflicts. There are many methods of communication that resolve conflict and are designed to build enduring and intimate relationships. They are simple and, most of all, effective. No matter what they are called or how many steps they have, they all operate on the principles designed to improve the way we listen and talk to each other.

Story Telling and Story Listening

We all have styles of communicating. Very few of us are able verbally to address our differences and needs, offer understanding and acceptance, and negotiate a compromise when needed.

Most of us grew up thinking that talking about feelings meant blaming the other person and complaining about what he or she has done to us. As adults, we carry this notion into relationships. Most of us express our feelings by criticizing the other person.

When we communicate, we become a patient and a therapist. We take turns telling a story about ourselves. The story teller is the patient who tells a story about his or her inner world, and the listener is the therapist, the audience. Like a good audience, the story listener is receptive and responsible for positive feedback.

Story telling reveals an inner world and tells how we feel inside. We can do this ourselves, by talking to a therapist or a friend. Even by talking to ourselves. The fact that we are social animals means that the most natural place to do this is within the context of our relationships. We build intimacy in a relationship by taking turns telling stories about how we feel inside.

Telling our personal stories is the paramount exchange of intimacy. When we find someone to listen to us tell about who we are as a person, it helps us discover who we are, what we need, and what we want. It helps fill the emptiness inside. It helps us gain a good sense of ourselves and build intimacy. We are less likely to go outside a marriage to find ourselves, or to find acceptance and validation.

Unlike conversations or arguments, story telling sessions are structured, and there are rules to follow: Set aside a story telling time. No more than twenty minutes. Take turns being a story teller and a story listener.

The rules are simple:

1. The story teller "tells a story" by relating a feeling about a problem. Use *I* to express your feelings and refrain from using *you*.
2. The story listener listens in a nice, empathic way. If *you* pops up, it is up to the story listener to bring the story teller back to *I*.
3. Do not continue when anger crops up.

Do this several times a week until the method of talking and listening to a story becomes a familiar and comfortable way of communicating.

TELLING A STORY

Story telling means telling about yourself, telling what you feel inside. You can even relate your feelings to your own personal history. Story telling in this way tells the other person about yourself. Use *I* instead of *you*. When we use *you,* we are not revealing an inner self but sending out blame. It also displaces responsibility, in effect making the other person responsible for our emotions.

Telling a story means revealing how you feel inside and then speculating upon where those feelings might have existed in our early life in order to gain insight.

The need to communicate an inner self is not easy. More often than not we want our mate to intuitively know what we need. We all yearn for our partner to be responsible for fixing us, for making us feel whole. For knowing what is wrong without our having to say it in words. For giving us good self-esteem. For fulfilling the needs within. But no one can be responsible for healing the wounds within, for making us feel separate yet strong. In the keen disappointment we feel when a marriage partner does not fill the emptiness inside, instead of finding a way to like what we are and where we are, instead of working on ourselves and the relationship, we run away. We withdraw. We escape into distance. We seek gratification. We go on a sexual detour.

Listening to a Story

The other half of the communication equation is story listening. Hearing the story our partner tells us is difficult because we are personally involved. We hear things that arouse our emotions in a primitive way. Listening is the professional art of therapy. Becoming a therapist in addition to becoming a husband or wife is not something we think of when we take our wedding vows, but it is in fact exactly what each of us needs to do once we take those vows.

Story listening means we listen to the story being told, and instead of taking it personally, instead of disputing whether the story is right or wrong, we just listen. We try to put ourselves in another's place. We may hear stories we don't like. We may hear facts or feelings we disagree with, and we may long to shout out in anger, but the difference in story listening is that we don't react. That does not mean we deny or change our thinking, but when we listen to the story, the only comments we make are ones that help the story teller tell us more of his or her own unique and personal story.

Like any good audience, story listeners should not act bored, angry, or barely tolerant. Simple expressions of responsiveness and understanding help the story teller reveal his or her own personal drama. Encouragement takes the form of a nod, a look, or a comment:

> *Go on.*
> *Oh?*
> *That's interesting.*
> *Really!*
> *Tell me more.*
> *I understand.*

Constructive questions help the story teller go into his or her inner life and explore what lies there in order to gain self-understanding.

> *Did you ever feel that way a long time ago?*
> *What does it feel like?*
> *How did you feel then?*
> *How does it feel now?*

In this way of listening, we don't fight about what we hear. We just listen. By listening to each other in this way, marital partners build intimacy.

The Sexual Connection

Restoring a sexual relationship that has been damaged or interrupted by an affair requires a recommitment to equality and trust. Both partners must acknowledge their role in the affair, as well as take the responsibility for rebuilding the sexual trust that has been shattered.

REESTABLISHING SEXUAL TRUST

The single most important element in reestablishing a sexual connection is overcoming the emotional *trauma* of sexual rejection. Sexual betrayal hits us at the core of who we are as sexual beings. Usually there are enough disturbances in the emotional relationship of a couple where one partner is involved in an affair to have put the other on edge. Anxiety, fear, and feelings of rejection so keenly interfere in our ability to enjoy a sexual relationship that unless these feelings are attended to, the sexual relationship suffers long after the affair is over.

What usually helps people who have been caught up in sexual betrayal is reassurance. Over and over and over again. I cannot stress this enough. Frequently the partner who has had the affair complains that he or she has already reassured. Already apologized. Already asked for forgiveness. I tell one and all the same thing: Do it again. The trauma of sexual rejection needs the soothing balm of good intentions, loving feelings, reassurance as to desirability, applied over and over to the sexual wound.

Time is a great healer. One of the ways sexual trust is reestablished is through the passage of time. Time that includes generous heapings of love, attention, and verbalization of our remorse and good intentions goes a long way. What goes even farther is the recognition that sexual fidelity is something that is demonstrated. When an affair is over, it has to be over. Any suspicion or cause for suspicion on the part of a partner undermines sexual security and sexual trust. The task of the partner who has taken a sexual detour is to establish a secure zone in which the marriage may thrive.

The task of those who have faced betrayal lies in learning to trust again. Forgiveness plays a key part. If we have truly forgiven our partner, we stop blaming and start picking up our share of building an intimate relationship that includes sexuality. Leaving the burden of our sexual insecurity forever on the back of a partner who engaged in an affair, as another facet of blame, only breaks the back of the marriage. Sexual affairs are not proof of undesirability, nor is fidelity a measure of sexual desirability. Sexual intimacy is something we build into our lives by working at it.

Taking responsibility for our share of rebuilding our sexual security involves allowing ourselves to be vulnerable to our partner. Reestablishing sexual intimacy means we must take a risk. Allowing the sexual connection to be repaired requires a leap of faith. When we have decided to reinvest in our marriage, the only thing we can do to demonstrate this willingness is to reengage in a sexual relationship. Sexual intimacy is reinforced and rebuilt in much the same way as emotional trust is restored in a *trustworthy* relationship.

Reestablishing sexual trust is the most difficult aspect of repairing a marriage after betrayal because it requires us to be vulnerable. Allowing ourselves once again to become exposed, especially in the sexual arena, is made easier by the continued assurances of our partner. The act of rebuilding takes time. For some, it is a difficult and halting process, one that only time and continued fidelity will establish. For others, it is a more easily accomplished step. For all, it involves demonstrating in the most intimate sense of the words the hope, love, and courage it takes to rebuild a marriage after a sexual detour.

REESTABLISHING SEXUAL AND PHYSICAL INTIMACY

Reintegrating sexual intimacy is something that naturally follows the reestablishment of emotional intimacy. However, sometimes we remain shy and we are afraid. I tell my patients that learning how to reestablish sexual intimacy can be made easier by using a partnering approach to physical pleasure. I urge them to spend a weekend away from home. Take a vacation. Plan romantic interludes. Or treat themselves to a course in sexuality right in the comfort of their own home.

To enhance physical intimacy, we must learn to distinguish sensuality from sexuality and learn to communicate clearly our sexual wishes. This is difficult under most circumstances, and even harder in the aftermath of an affair. What makes it easier is to use the tried-and-true approach recommended by sex therapists: sensate focus exercises created by Masters and Johnson.

Sensate focus centers around physical exercises that teach couples how to take turns giving and receiving physical pleasure. Basically, what most sex therapists teach is the art of the caress. Tactile pleasure is recalled and relearned. The method is easy to understand and implement and helps ease fear of performance.

First of all, it is important to recognize that sexual functioning is a phenomenon of vasocongestion, an engorgement of blood vessels, tissues, and organs, and is not a measure of true love. This state of plumbing is the nature of physical sexual responsivity. It is triggered by erotic stimulation, whether touch, sight, sound, smell, memories, or fantasies.

During sex, the erotic trigger sends blood into the sexual tissues of the body. An erection occurs when more blood drains into the penis than can leave it. This allows the penis to penetrate the vagina. In females, arousal similarly prepares the vagina so that it becomes more receptive and can more easily accept penetration by the male organ.

Many things, both emotional and physical, can interfere with the process. Focus on performance interferes with arousal, and this is especially true when sexual infidelity has occurred and insecurities peak. Performance anxiety drains blood away from the genitals. An unhurried and loving manner helps ensure successful sex. Impulsive, spontaneous sex is fine if it works, but for most of us good planning and attention to every detail works better.

The first phase of sensate focus requires abstinence from actual sexual contact. This removes the performance anxiety from goal-oriented sex. In this exercise, we focus on sensuality. We are free to caress, massage, kiss—anything we want except touch the genital area. We take turns simply stroking the body of our partner, communicating what feels nice. The goal is not of sexual arousal or performance. The goal is simply to enjoy the pleasant sensation of touch.

In the second phase the same process is repeated, only now, sexual arousal of the genitals may be included. But no intercourse is *required*. There is nothing to worry about. Orgasm is not the end result. This phase is one of sexual stimulation with no goal other than that each partner take turns bringing sexual pleasure and excitement to the other. Somewhere along the way, sensate focus will help reinforce, enhance, and reestablish sexual trust and intimacy.

Chapter Seventeen

❧❧

Growing Whole

> *Oft-times nothing profits more*
> *Than self-esteem, grounded on just and right*
> *Well managed.*
>
> —JOHN MILTON,
> *PARADISE LOST*

❧ While our development is most active in the formative years of infancy, childhood, and even adolescence, in adulthood we continue to grow. The rate is slower but the process is the same. In *The Empathic Imagination* by Albert Marguiles, Milan Kundera's notion of living on a Planet of Inexperience is marvelously explored. In this book, the idea that the creation of the world did not occur at the beginning of time, but occurs each day, is put forth. Every day we are faced with new dramas, new challenges, as infants, children, adults, partners, and parents. We even enter old age as children, not knowing what we face or what lies ahead.

The drama of living with the unforeseeable future is never felt more keenly than during the catastrophic events in our lives such as grave illness, death, and the end of an important relationship. The wake of a sexual detour represents, for some of us, this same kind of personal crisis. For all of us, it represents a crisis of opportunity. Rarely are we prepared for the forces that rock us, and we know little of how to achieve recovery. Crisis, however, because of the intense attention to the acute problem at hand, brings heightened awareness. Change blows into our lives, and old and new shift. One door closes and another opens. The emotional jolt of a personal crisis can motivate us to actively seek out new ways of understanding ourselves in order to ensure that the past does not repeat itself. Growth and maturity are often born of painful times.

Maturity is not, as the word may imply, age. Rather, it refers to a whole, intact, and separate person who can function as an individual capable of insight and of self-understanding. A mature adult can tolerate frustration and does not need to act out in self-destructive ways. When we are mature, key issues around abandonment and loss, or engulfment and control, are *under control*. These issues are not absent from our emotional lives, but they are under control. This means that we are capable of merging in a relationship where negotiation and compromise exist. Our expectations become more realistic. Our self-esteem is a palpable presence within ourselves and we are able to see our partners for who they are, not as the figures transference might make them into. We are better able to function as good partners when we grow more whole.

Emotional Vision

Growing whole requires purposeful action versus passive reaction. It is a process of gaining emotional vision, of opening up our inner selves, and revealing to ourselves not just what we want but also *why*.

Emotional vision reflects the capacity for knowing our problems and where they come from. As a whole, intact person, we have the ability to distinguish between problems coming from inside ourselves or from outside reality. One result of inner vision is that we are less likely to blame our partner for internal issues that interfere with feeling good about ourselves or for the problems that arise in our relationships. This responsibility for our self brings us closer to solving problems and getting what we want out of life, and farther from the kind of acting-out behavior that results in a sexual detour.

Many of my patients suffer from the mistaken notion that what ails and provokes anxiety comes from the outside and is dependent upon the action of others. Whether that is true or not is less of an issue than the fact that there are many things we cannot control. Blame is useless because we have limited control over certain realities, and we cannot change anyone else. We can change only ourselves and our reactions to situations and in this way attain a measure of balance and control.

We discard blame and accept responsibility by turning to an inner world. Becoming intimate with our inner world is a healing process. Self-awareness builds our self-esteem. When we acknowledge all our strengths and weaknesses, we no longer need to hide parts of ourselves in shame or out of fear. Shame hurts. We can't change if shame keeps us hidden from ourselves. The part of ourselves that needs to grow whole is this hidden part. One of the ways to let go of shame is to come to love the little child that you were shamed into believing wasn't *good enough* but really *is*. You have to raise that little child all over again. It is the part of yourself that you put away. Emotional vision frees us from the shame and gives us a self to share.

Accepting ourselves means taking responsibility for who we are, what we do, and the choices we make. This is the hallmark of an authentic person who demonstrates pride in himself or herself.

Becoming authentic, having a whole sense of ourselves, enables us to establish an *intimate communication* with ourselves and others. Revealing ourselves to another, who in turn accepts us for who we are, builds more strength and further increases our self-esteem. Intimacy helps us develop new skills, set goals, take risks, and fulfill our wishes. Self-knowledge and intimacy become a self-fulfilling prophecy by reinforcing positive skills.

I stress with my patients that an inner journey brings an achievement. The process itself is a victory of which they can feel proud. It is not easy to pierce the veil of an inner self. Some of us see ourselves only through rose-colored glasses. Others with a dark, somber, and critical eye. Some of us operate in total blindness. Sometimes it is only through a personal crisis that we are able to put ourselves into perspective. That is why a sexual detour represents such an important window of opportunity. The victory of engaging in the process and gaining emotional knowledge is restorative. It is a healing and hard-won gift.

Crisis is a fork in the road. No matter what the past has wrought or what the future holds, we cannot step into the same river twice. We will be able to move only as changed individuals in altered states. Our experiences will have impact upon us and those connected to us. We will have scars, but scar tissue is said to be stronger.

Finding Our Conscious Self

In order to move forward purposefully, to change anything in ourselves or in our lives, we have to tackle the job of growing whole by understanding ourselves first and then by translating the illuminating force of understanding *into a conscious act*. If we want to change

anything, fix anything, we *have to do it consciously*. Only our conscious self can override the powerful motivation of our unconscious
wishes and fears. When we gain the power of conscious choice, we
flex an invisible muscle. This strength gives us the courage for free
choice. When what we cannot see becomes visible, doors open. We
reach a watershed. Transformation becomes possible with understanding when we know *why*.

Why has a peculiar power. It releases us from what we may have
ordinarily thought, or even from the constraint of what we should
be thinking or feeling. It allows us to explore our inner world in
much the same way as we explored the world around us as children. Childhood is an endless chorus of whys. Why this. Why that.
Why everything. My mother, either because she did not know the
answers to my endless list of whys or simply couldn't be bothered,
developed an easy answer for every why in the world:

Y is a crooked letter.

What that said to me was ultimately it didn't matter why. Why
was a frivolous pastime. *What mattered was what I ended up doing.*

I've spent the better part of my adult life trying to help people discover the answer to their own whys and then helping them
finally *do*. At the end of the day, the beginning of the journey, we
have to stop asking and start doing. We have to go someplace.
However, unless we know why, we won't know where we're
going. Asking helps us discover who we are and thus gives us a
road map. Unless we have the road map of knowing who we are,
and what we really need and want, we may take the wrong turn
and somehow find ourselves off the beaten path and once again in
an obscure wood.

Having attainable hopes and finding fulfillment of dreams is the promise growing whole holds. The difference between growing whole and hiding on a sexual detour is knowing ourselves more honestly. It is a struggle to go through guilt and forgiveness, feel loneliness and fear, or experience our own weakness as we fight to grow whole. It is a process wherein we learn who we really are and what we need. We grow emotional muscle as we search ourselves. The painful process we go through in the aftermath of a sexual detour can be one of growth.

The process of growing whole takes place in three arenas of our lives:

EMOTIONAL ARENA

We experience ourselves most intensely in the emotional sphere. By looking at our relationships with others, we can see a picture of who we are and how others influence how we feel about ourselves. This examination of the emotional world is vital, both in childhood and throughout adulthood. A good sense of self-esteem reinforced in positive relationships allows us to feel vitality, creativity, and bonded to others. Self-esteem grows out of how we experience the world and how the world reflects our actions.

PHYSICAL ARENA

Physical movement and pleasure in our bodies are of paramount importance in feeling whole. When we can take care of our bodies, use our bodies creatively and for pleasure, we feel better about ourselves emotionally.

INTELLECTUAL ARENA

How we experience the world and function in the world vis-à-vis our interests and our careers can allow us to grow. Intellectual stimulation teaches us to grow in unexpected ways and helps us find avenues of change. The pursuit of interests uniquely our own can help us define ourselves and structure purpose into our lives.

Feeling whole involves two steps in all these three arenas of our lives. The two steps involve:

1. *Reflection:* taking a journey within
2. *Action:* to reinforce and establish what we have learned in reflection

Step 1: Reflection

EMOTIONAL ARENA

1. Make a commitment.

The first step is actively to commit to the pursuit of self-knowledge. Like other important commitments in our lives, this endeavor is not demonstrated in word, but in deed. The pursuit of self-awareness involves the commitment of:

time

Set aside some time as if it were a bag of gold. The amount is up to you. It's your time. If you value your time, you will set aside more, not less, for this crucial journey. Nothing is more precious to us than time, and nothing is more important than to use some of it for ourselves. We can make the best use of our time if we can stretch it out and use it grain by grain, very deliberately. The amount of the time set aside, five minutes or fifty, matters less than a scrupulous adherence to the process. Every day, no matter where, no matter what, take out a measure of time and set it aside, as if on a shelf.

2. *Focus.*

The second step involves how we use the time set aside. This time should be used only for one deliberate purpose:

take the time to focus on your inner self

Let me distinguish between taking time for yourself and taking time for your self. Time for yourself might be reading the paper, shopping, taking a walk, hiking, exercising, taking a nap. It's a treat. Like a bubble bath. A quiet corner with a good book. Time for yourself is something to indulge in that feels enjoyable. Time for your *self*, on the other hand, is focusing on your inner self. It is a meeting of your minds. Your conscious mind connecting, insofar as that is possible, to your unconscious mind. The hardest sphere to reflect upon is this inner emotional world.

There are many ways we can focus on ourselves. We can think, look, talk, question, sort, or sift. Reflection reveals the fears, wishes, and dreams of our innermost self. We take out our hopes and dreams and think about what they are, where they came from, and why. We examine our fears in the same way. We think. And we rethink.

PHYSICAL ARENA

There are physical manifestations of exploring your emotional arena in a way that utilizes your physical gifts.

1. *Write.*

Many people find that one of the easiest and most rewarding ways to reflect is to write in a daily journal. Each day, the journal is used as the repository for thoughts and houses what we might glean from the rummaging we do in the basement of the self.

2. Look.

Use your sense of visual awareness. I tell many of my patients who are fortunate enough to have family photo albums or videos of their childhood to use them. Look and remember. Notice what feelings they evoke. Like music from a bygone day, these strike chords of nostalgia and provide missing pieces of an inner self we have drummed out of our awareness. When visual memory clicks in, it brings emotional memory and emotional knowledge. The people in the pictures are still alive within us, no matter how our appearance has changed. Noticing the similarities between the past and present gives us a clearer picture of the patterns of our feelings and behavior.

Another way to look inside is by looking outside. A patient of mine uses a hand mirror and studies her face every day for at least five minutes. She is drawn, she says, not so much into the lines on her face as into the crevices of the past. Memories come forth, feelings and experiences are evoked, as the face in the mirror becomes secondary to the thoughts about herself. She uses her mirror as a gateway into herself. It is almost as if the intense reflection operates as self-hypnosis. In self-hypnosis, any device that focuses the mind and sets us free from external distraction gives us a ticket to time travel.

3. Talk.

Improve your ability to communicate verbally. Talking is a good vehicle to use for a journey within. We can uncover our cover stories and discover who we really are by talking to someone about ourselves. And no, it does not need to be a therapist. Needless to say, it is an expensive situation to set up enough time for this project with a professional listener. Talking to someone each and every day is complicated, even with a partner who is willing to lend an ear and a nod now and then. What that leaves us with is talking to ourselves. Not a bad idea. For openers, talking out loud forces us to play two roles. When we talk, we become listeners. In listening to ourselves, we automatically turn the questions around and are forced to ponder ourselves a bit more. This may feel embarrassing at first, particularly if someone else is in the room or nearby. So try the shower, and instead of singing, talk to yourself.

4. Listen.

Practice what Theodore Reik called listening with the third ear—to others as well as yourself. Wake up to your sleep self and listen to what you are saying. An interesting route into the inner self is to write down what your sleep self is talking about. "A dream is a wish your heart makes when you're fast asleep." The Disney refrain echoes through our childhood, but although it's close, it's not quite correct. Dreams arise not from the heart, but from what is going on in our present-day lives and from unconscious yearnings, fears, and unresolved conflicts.

Dreams can tell us a great deal about ourselves because they are the unconscious representations of what is going on inside. The unconscious is creative, melodramatic, and accurate. Dreams give us instant, clear, and important information. The information is precise because we never dream about anything that applies to anyone else. Dreams are self-

centered and self-serving. No matter how small and insignificant the detail is, we dream about what is important to *us*.

The vividness of dreams feels as real as conscious life.
When horrors befall, and dreams are frightful, we usually
awaken with a start, heart pounding. Sometimes they are so
vivid we cannot tell the dream from reality, yet when we
awaken, dreams can evaporate like smoke. Usually, when we
try to grasp at the wisps of the dream with our conscious
mind they elude us, trailing back off into the unconscious
recesses of an inner world. Some are so strong that they stay
with us for hours. Most of us want to forget nightmares. And
why not? But they may articulate for us that which we are
unable to tell ourselves. They can let us know what we are
afraid of, and even why.

Dreams are the way the brain discharges, processes, and
translates the daytime data. Some dreams clearly reflect this
conscious daytime sensory input. We have snippets of dreams
countless times a night of which we are unaware as we rid
ourselves of daytime debris. We also have more lengthy, intri-
cate, complicated dreams wherein we solve problems or
replay them. Dreams can reoccur for years, echoing the key
problems and chronic anxieties of our lives.

In light of the fact that there is a performance nightly,
right in the comfort of your own bedroom, attend the show.
During this investigatory phase, keep regular sleep hours. A
bath before bed will relax your body. Keep a pad of paper and
a pen next to your bed. When you awaken from a dream, or in
the mornings, try to remember the fragments and quickly
write them down. Don't be dissuaded if you find that you've

written gibberish. Eventually, somewhere, a word or a phrase will bring back something from the dream that may enlighten your day journey as well.

5. *Ask.*

Connect yourself to others and to yourself. Growing whole is a lifetime affair. No one can be so presumptuous as to believe it ever stops, that we arrive at adulthood and are finished. Our growth continues, and ensuring our development requires our attention. All we have to do is look at the human body and our neurobiological interiors to bear witness to the complexities of existence. An inward journey helps us track another dimension of our growth and development.

One way to journey inward is to ask ourselves questions about ourselves and our relationships. These are questions that many of you will be able to answer in some detail and others only sketchily. If answers are not forthcoming, take the time over and over to ask again. You will need a paper and pencil or handy keyboard. Sit down and begin with a look at your family of origin. Here are some sample questions:

Family of Origin
How did your parents relate to you?
Were you allowed to develop a true inner sense of
   what you felt?
Did you grow up with the feeling that your parents
   communicated?
What was your mother's view of love?
What was your father's view of love?

Did you grow up believing in a prince in the guise of
a regular guy?

Did you grow up waiting for a princess to come
along?

Were you taught that love is chemistry?

Were you taught that love endures through daily action?

Marriage

When did you get married?

Why did you get married?

What was your life like before you married?

Did you want to escape your home?

Were you hoping that you would be rescued?

Can you answer these questions for your mate, and if
not why not?

What do you still like about your partner?

What do you still like about yourself?

Are you the parent or the child in your relationship?

Do you want to change?

How do you think you can change?

Sexual Detour

If an affair was hoped for or acted upon, what was
going on inside of you?

What was going on inside of your marital partner?

If you didn't know the answer to the above question,
why not?

Were you afraid to confront your fear? Hurt? Anger?

Did you choose a partner in an affair who had something you did not?

What was it that attracted you to the partner in an
   affair?

How did your affair make you feel about yourself?

Did your mate see you less favorably than did a partner in an affair?

What did you hope an affair would give you?

What can you do to give that to yourself?

INTELLECTUAL ARENA

1. *Take inventory.*

Somewhere in the middle of life, beset by measurements of
everything down to grams and milligrams, we may get the
notion that living would be done better under a whole different rule. Perhaps the error is in the concept. Measure is different somehow from measurement. Taking the measure of a
life feels more whole than taking measurements. More lasting
and worthwhile. More worth calculating. In taking stock of
who and what we are, we may find out more about ourselves:
characteristics, aspirations, talents, predispositions, inclina-
tions. It is an inventory of what comprises the person we feel
we are and think we are. It goes without saying that this inventory should be an honest self-appraisal as well as an exhaustive
one. It should, in words, give a clear picture of the physical,
emotional, and intellectual beings we are. We may be surprised at how many assets we have that we took as liabilities.

We may have mistaken ideas of the way we are perceived
by those around us. We can use intimate friends, work partners, and casual acquaintances in our lives to help give us a
picture of ourselves. If we check our inventory against theirs,

we will discover more about who we are. Like a mosaic, these tiny fragments reflect part of the whole self. This is in some ways a reality check against our own denial. Remember, no right or wrong here. Simply information so that we can learn more about who we are and who we might want to become.

Ask the questions about yourself from a number of different people. Use the same type of questions. This is a personal survey. If a majority of people describe you as quiet and withdrawn and you don't perceive yourself that way, what does that mean? Perhaps it means you are afraid to admit you are shy. To hear any criticism may be too painful. Asking for a critique of yourself may mean taking an emotional risk, but we can garner very worthwhile information about ourselves in this way by creating a road map we can follow to find ourselves. Some questions to ask might be:

How would you describe me?
Do I seem easily irritated?
Am I friendly and sociable, or withdrawn?
What three characteristics describe me best?

2. Determine priorities and set goals.

In discarding what is unimportant and determining our priorities, we reveal more about who we are and what we represent. What is important to us defines who we are. Hone your self. Sort and sift through what you can do without and what is of real value. Discard what is not really important to you. We usually know what to trim with our physical selves. Fat applies not only to inches but to the dimensions of the inner world as well.

Emotional tone is as important as muscle tone. This sorting and sifting will bring into focus your priorities and values, and allow you to set reasonable goals and hold expectations of yourself that you can successfully accomplish. Some questions you might ask of yourself are:

What do I want to build in myself?
What strengths do I want to encourage?
What do I want to discard?

There comes a point, which is different for each person, when what we learn has to be put into practice. Sitting and staring at our navel may bring about inner enlightenment and make our lives infinitely more peaceable, but the chances are, unless we *do something,* unless we put knowledge into action, nothing will change. The vehicle through which we change ourselves, or our lives, is *behavior.* After the first step of reflection, we arrive at the second step of growing whole: *action.*

Step 2: Action

With emotional knowledge we discover more potential in ourselves and our lives than we had ever hoped to find. Inevitably, this knowledge brings loss as well. Knowledge dispels fantasy. Self-knowledge, which reveals and enables an enriching and hopeful future, also uncovers the futility of fantasy. The loss is sad and painful when we discover that our wishes are not congruent with reality. We may want what is self-destructive. We may want things we cannot have. Wanting is easy. Giving up and growing whole is hard.

Growth not only involves learning but also requires shedding and reconciling ourselves to the losses real life demands of us. In the aftermath of an affair, we need to restore hope, rebuild strength, replace illusion, and employ methods to start anew. Change requires courage and an active change of behavior. Action and doing breed self-esteem. If you find yourself paralyzed and unable to take action, go back to Step 1 and search out what fears prevent you from taking action. Then, come back to Step 2 and push them through, being kind and accepting of yourself in the process. Change doesn't happen in a day. If you want to change, you will.

Emotional Arena

1. Stop the behavior.
No matter what kind of destructive behavior plagues your life or hampers your recovery, GIVE IT UP. This is the starting point for any kind of change. Destructive behavior is anything that perpetuates situations in which we find ourselves abused or in which we are the abuser. Abuse is something we are addicted to, whether it is sexual acting out, alcohol, drugs, compulsive overeating, or rage reactions. Whatever the negative behavior, giving it up means just one thing: STOP. Stop the old behavior and begin a new one. The first step comes with the decision, but in order to solidify changed behavior, we need to understand its roots. Above all, we may need to have help from the outside.

2. *Reach out for support.*

To solidify change in behavior, reach out for support. The climb toward recovery from physical and emotional crisis is often hard and long, and we all need help. Friends and family can lend crucial help. If you prefer the kindness of strangers, they will become your extended family. Twelve-step support groups provide enormous help. I am an avid supporter of such groups. A support group helps you to see yourself without shame and without the prejudice of others' opinions. It helps you find a new, enlarged opinion of yourself. Support groups are made up of those who have been there, have been helped by others, and are eager to pass along what they have learned. When you reveal the shame you may feel about who you are, a supportive atmosphere where you are accepted can begin actively to raise your self-esteem. It helps you stop the behavior—for good.

The origin of self-esteem comes from the way we are seen. If we have suffered from emotional trauma—meaning more negative experiences than positive ones—we can become plagued by shame and keep that part of ourselves hidden, thereby preventing change. In order to like yourself with all your flaws so that transformation is possible, acceptance and understanding are crucial. Standing up in a support group and stating what makes you feel ashamed diminishes the shame. By sharing the secrets about yourself that you are ashamed of, you can evolve and thereby grow more whole. When we pass through the stages of accepting responsibility, blame, anger, and resentment give way to self-love and growth. We cannot love another if we cannot love ourselves.

There are support groups for every crisis imaginable, and
many meetings are listed in the newspapers.

3. Take an emotional risk.
This does not mean *put yourself at risk*. Taking an emotional risk
means challenging yourself to deal with your own particular
personal issues. Revealing your vulnerabilities and engaging in
an emotional life despite the disappointments and pain of the
past are emotional risks. Fear of being hurt and feeling
strongly should not stop you from embracing feelings. Risk
passion. Employ trust. Express your vulnerabilities. Work out
the emotional kinks by risking emotional change even though
this may involve fear and loss. Giving up illusion is risking
change. Resolve whatever your particular issue is. We all have
painful personal issues we avoid. We may feel insecure and
unsure. This might mean trusting again. This might mean
allowing ourselves to feel vulnerable. This might mean
redefining our feelings about expressing sexuality. We may
want to hide emotionally for what we've convinced ourselves
are a thousand good reasons. Don't. Do it. Be it.

4. Respect individuality.
Whatever your personal quotient is, feel it, be it, do it. Wear
a suit and tie to sleep if you prefer. Cherish your individuality.
This does not mean defending destructive, immature, or
unkind behavior. It simply means appreciating your unique-
ness and liking yourself. Along with respecting your own individuality comes an appreciation of the right of others to have
a distinct and separate identity different from your own. We
are all separate individuals, unique in our own way, and should

both give and receive respect from those who share our lives. Therefore, if your mate wants to wear a suit or tie to sleep, respect it as you would wish your self to be respected as well.

5. Be intimate.

Intimacy is an active commitment. It requires an ongoing effort to build intimacy into a relationship. Intimacy insists that we know ourselves, respect ourselves, and demonstrate trustworthiness. When we take responsibility for our actions and eliminate blame from our lives, we both give and garner respect. Liking, love, and intimacy grow and require that we are willing to go the distance in order to establish them in our lives. Put intimacy into action. Intimacy as an active commitment may mean risking something in the face of fear. Defining what intimacy means to you and to your partner helps you build intimacy into your lives. Ask yourselves the following questions:

> How is intimacy defined for you and your partner?
> Is intimacy defined the same for both of you?
> Is intimacy defined sexually?
> Is intimacy defined by feelings of closeness or trust?

If you are confused as to what intimacy means, rethink the issue and then with your mate engage in the following exercise:

> Reveal to each other the ways intimacy is present in
> the relationship.
> Reveal to each other how the concept of intimacy has
> changed during the course of the marriage.

Reevaluate your definition of intimacy and how you
are building it into your life. Remember, growing
whole is a lifetime affair.

PHYSICAL ARENA

1. Move your body.

Engage in some form of regular exercise. Stretching counts.
Do it alone or convince a buddy to motivate you. If that doesn't
get your body moving, enroll in a class that requires you to
move your body in some way, shape, or form. The list, from
yoga to community sports, is endless.

2. Take care of your body.

It goes without saying that regular medical and dental care is
important, but often in the crisis of our lives, we neglect the
basics. Get the basics checked without delay no matter what
else is going on in your life. If you abuse your body, get help
from a support group so you can take better care of yourself.

3. Pamper your body.

Indulge your body in special ways that feel good to you. There
is no better or more important time to pay special attention
to yourself in a physical way than during an emotional crisis.
Soaking baths, invigorating showers, massaging oils and
lotions, and special attention to appearance give a sense of
physical and emotional well-being.

4. *Play with your body.*

Do you have shame about your body that inhibits you from playfulness, either in bed, in clothes, in sports, or in secret? Broaden your perspectives and recognize that your body is the temple of your soul. Worship it . . . playfully.

INTELLECTUAL ARENA

1. *Play.*

We are social animals, and in the tumult of a fractured personal life, we may have ignored the boisterous flow of life that nourishes the human need for social contact. Renew and enrich friendships. Learn to play in whatever way works for you. Some blare rock music; others tune in to soft classical. Tap-dance or dig in your garden. Paint the walls. Read the newspapers. Listen to the news. Have a conversation. Engage in life in a manner that encourages social contact and play.

2. *Learn.*

Learning something new engenders stimulation, enrichment, and freedom. Whether it is knitting or a new language, the opportunities open to us through community education sources are infinite. Physical tasks or intellectual pursuits give us avenues of exploration that open up both inner and outer worlds.

3. *Help.*

Step outside of yourself and help someone else. The world is bigger than our own personal crisis. Some of the darkest hours can be brightened by the light we carry to others. The volunteer world is an honorable place to spend a few hours. It can be as simple as helping the elderly person next door or reading a book to a classroom of children.

Conclusion

This brings to a close the easy part. Mine. It's always easy telling people what to do. The hard part is actually doing it, and it is twofold.

First is the continuing struggle of trying to understand ourselves. It is an ongoing attempt to recognize that there are issues within us all that continue to thwart our desires and sabotage our efforts by providing us with cover stories instead of the real insights that make us whole. These inner wounds and the avoidance of feeling them are issues with which we all struggle. We all want soothing and a strong sense of self-identity. We all have to deal with the fear of closeness and intimacy and struggle with issues of abandonment and control. We all carry the emotional baggage of the past and unwittingly transfer it onto those in our present-day lives. We all suffer from the emotional wounds that interfere with self-esteem. Importantly, we all hold the elements of repair for one another in the understanding and empathy we can lend and in the ways we can learn to accept ourselves.

Second is the continuing effort of building an intimate relationship through both word and deed. We can enhance the course of our emotional lives with the vehicle of communication. Understanding ourselves and relating to one another as empathetic partners promise a path leading toward lasting intimacy, instead of sexual detours.

A sexual detour is a wake-up call telling us that something is going on inside of ourselves of which we are not aware. This alarm warns us that we are not following a line of emotional sight, but are deviating from a more direct route in an unconscious search to gain something we desperately need. If we heed this call and look deeply into ourselves, an affair can become a crisis of opportunity wherein we can develop the internal vision needed to grow whole and become capable of having enriching intimacy in our lives.

Love and grief are different sides of the same coin. It is only by doing the work of growing whole that we can understand and savor the bittersweet nature of our humanity. The greatest gift an effort to grow whole brings is allowing us to stretch and gain the inner vision that offers us potential for our future: the ability to become intimate.

The journey within and the intimate connection to another take courage and commitment. Dedication. Sexual detours may be enchanting. Divorce may prove easy. The road to intimacy is hard and long, but it leads to a place we all long for. It is coming home to the strength, peace, love, and security of an enduring intimate relationship. So go on, have an affair. With yourself.

Bibliography

Adler, Jerry. "Adultery, a New Furor over an Old Sin." *Newsweek*, September 30, 1996, 54–60.

Atcheson, Richard. "Oh, Such a Hungry Yearning." *Lear's*, February 1991, 55–57 +.

Bach, George R., and Ronald M. Deutsch. *Pairing: How to Achieve Genuine Intimacy*. New York: Avon Books, 1970.

Baumgold, Julie. "Why She, Personally, Won't." *Mirabella*, March/April 1996, 80.

Beattie, Melody. *Codependent No More: How to Stop Controlling Others and Start Caring for Yourself*. New York: Harper & Row, 1987.

Bennetts, Leslie. "Cheating." *Ladies' Home Journal*, September 1996, 76–80.

Broderick, Carlfred. *Couples: How to Confront Problems and Maintain Loving Relationships*. New York: Simon & Schuster, 1979.

Brzeczek, Richard, Elizabeth Brzeczek, and Sharon De Vita. *Addicted to Adultery: How We Saved Our Marriage/How You Can Save Yours*. New York: Bantam Books, 1989.

Campbell, Joseph. *The Power of Myth with Bill Moyers*. Edited by Betty Sue Flowers. New York: Doubleday, 1988.

Carter, Stephen L. "Falling Out of Love." *Mirabella*, March/April 1996, 79.

DeSalvo, Louise. "Fidelity—What's Sex Got to Do With It?" *Mirabella*, March/April 1996, 88.

Ehrenreich, Barbara. "Why It Might Be." *Mirabella*, March/April 1996, 78–79.

Farney, Dennis. "Today's Twentysomethings: Realistic, Living in Present." *The Wall Street Journal*, July 6, 1998, A26.

Flook, Maria. "Fidelity and the Long-Distance Marriage." *Mirabella*, March/April 1996, 85–86.

Gaylin, Willard, and Ethel Person, eds. *Passionate Attachments: Thinking About Love*. New York: The Free Press, 1988.

Glass, Shirley. "Vows." *Psychology Today*, July/August 1998, 35–42+.

Goldberg, Arnold, ed. *The Psychology of the Self: A Casebook*. Collaborated by Heinz Kohut, M.D. New York: International Universities Press, 1978.

Hempel, Amy. "Flirting With Disaster." *Mirabella*, March/April 1996, 81.

Hendrix, Harville. *Getting the Love You Want: A Guide For Couples*. New York: Harper & Row, 1988.

Heyn, Dalma. "Why Women Are Always to Blame." *Mirabella*, March/April 1996, 86–87.

Johnson, Robert A. *We: Understanding the Psychology of Romantic Love*. San Francisco: Harper & Row, 1983.

Jordan-Smith, Paul. "Epicycle I: Oedipus." *Parabola: Myth and the Quest for Meaning*, 2, no. 4 (1985): 46–48.

Krantzler, Mel. "The 6 Stages of Marriage." *Good Housekeeping*, June 1981, 24+.

Margulies, Alfred. *The Empathic Imagination*. New York: W. W. Norton, 1989.

Mark, Bonnie S., and James A. Incorvaia, eds. *The Handbook of Infant, Child, and Adolescent Psychotherapy: New Directions in Integrative Treatment, Reiss-David Child Study Center*. Volume 2. Northvale, NJ: Jason Aronson, 1997.

Marks, Jane. "I Had a Fling with My Boss." *Ladies' Home Journal*, July 1998, 15–16+.

McDevitt, John B., and Calvin F. Settlage, eds. *Separation-Individuation: Essays in Honor of Margaret S. Mahler*. New York: International Universities Press, 1971.

McKay, Matthew, and Patrick Fanning. *Self Esteem: The Ultimate Program for Self-Help*. New York: MJF Books, 1987.

Milkman, Harvey, and Stanley Sunderwith. *Craving for Ecstasy: The Consciousness and Chemistry of Escape*. New York: Free Press, 1987.

Miller, Alice. *The Drama of the Gifted Child: How Narcissistic Parents Form and Deform the Emotional Lives of Their Talented Children.* Translated by Ruth Ward. New York: Basic Books, 1981.

Miller, Sherod, Elam W. Nunnally, and Daniel B. Wackman. *Couple Communication I: Talking Together.* Littleton, CO: Interpersonal Communication Programs, 1979.

Myers, Michael F. "Residency and Marriage: Oil and Water?" *Medical Economics,* June 15, 1998, 152–56.

Nemiroff, Robert A., Alan Sugarman, and Alvin Robbins, eds. *On Loving, Hating, and Living Well: The Public Psychoanalytic Lectures of Ralph R. Greenson, M.D.* Monograph 2. Madison, CT: International Universities Press, 1992.

Owens, Michele, and Gerald Coble. "The Wandering Wife in Film." *Mirabella,* March/April 1996, 82–83.

Paul, Jordan, and Margaret Paul. *Do I Have to Give Up Me to Be Loved By You?* Minnesota: Compcare Publishers, 1983.

Person, Ethel Spector. *Dreams of Love and Fateful Encounters: The Power of Romantic Passion.* New York: W. W. Norton, 1988.

Pittman, Frank S. *Man Enough: Fathers, Sons, and the Search for Masculinity.* New York: Putnam, 1993.

———. *Private Lies: Infidelity and Betrayal of Intimacy.* New York: W. W. Norton, 1990.

Reik, Theodor. *The Need to Be Loved.* New York: Farrar, Straus, 1963.

Rose, Phyllis. "Anna Karenina, the Patron Saint of Adulteresses." *Mirabella,* March/April 1996, 82–83.

Ryan, Michael. "Why He Never Will Again." *Mirabella,* March/April 1996, 80–81.

Sagan, Dorion. "Gender Specifics: Why Women Aren't Men." *The New York Times,* June 21, 1998, pp. 1, 20.

Scarf, Maggie. *Intimate Partners: Patterns in Love and Marriage.* New York: Random House, 1987.

———. "What a Triangle Can Do for a Marriage." *Mirabella,* March/April 1996, 87–88.

Scharff, David E. *The Sexual Relationship: An Object Relations View of Sex and the Family*. Northvale, NJ: Jason Aronson, 1998.

Shapiro, Michael. "Q. Why Do We Fall in Love." *Mirabella*, November 1992, 32.

Sherven, Judith, and James Sniechowski. *The New Intimacy: Discovering the Magic at the Heart of Your Differences*. Deerfield Beach, FL: Health Communications, 1997.

Smiley, Jane. "Why It's Not Worth It." *Mirabella*, March/April 1996, 78–79.

Solomon, Marion F. *Narcissism and Intimacy: Love and Marriage in an Age of Confusion*. New York: W. W. Norton, Inc., 1989.

Spring, Janis Abrahms. *After the Affair: Healing the Pain and Rebuilding Trust When a Partner Has Been Unfaithful*. New York: HarperCollins, 1997.

Stern, Daniel N. *The Interpersonal World of the Infant: A View from Psychoanalysis and Developmental Psychology*. New York: Basic Books, 1985.

Tannen, Deborah. *Talking From 9 to 5, Women and Men in the Workplace: Language, Sex and Power*. New York: Avon Books, 1994.

Thurman, Judith. "Monogamy, the French Version." *Mirabella*, March/April 1996, 84–85.

Viorst, Judith. *Necessary Losses: The Loves, Illusions, Dependencies and Impossible Expectations That All of Us Have to Give Up in Order to Grow*. New York: Fawcett, 1986.

Viscott, David. *I Love You, Let's Work It Out*. New York: Simon & Schuster, 1987.

Weiner-Davis, Michele. *A Woman's Guide to Changing Her Man (Without His Even Knowing It)*. New York: Golden Books, 1998.

Wheelis, Allen. *How People Change*. New York: Harper & Row, 1973.

Wolfe, Linda. *Playing Around: Women and Extramarital Sex*. New York: William Morrow, 1975.

Yalom, Irvin D. *Love's Executioner & Other Tales of Psychotherapy*. New York: HarperCollins, 1989.

I believe that it is through connection and interaction that one gains a more varied awareness and deeper capacity to live in the world. In my opinion, connection is about reciprocity. Sometimes one gives and sometimes one takes. The ability to do both provides for an enduring and intimate exchange.

The essential aspects of an integrated self are the mind, body, and the spirit interwoven and balanced one with the other. I can honestly state that my work with people has helped them to transform their lives. I know it has transformed mine. No one changes overnight. It took me a long time to define myself. It was through my choices, both my successes and failures, that I have been able to find a safe place within myself to create and prosper. I hope I can help my readers to do the same.

DR. HOLLY HEIN was born in Brooklyn, New York, the daughter of two very accomplished New York attorneys. She was educated at Dana Hall, a boarding school in Wellesley, Massachusetts. Dr. Hein received her graduate degree from New York University, School of Social Work, and received her doctorate from the Institute of Clinical Social Work in Berkeley, California. She also has postgraduate degrees from the Institute of Ego-Psychology in New York and the Institute for Contemporary Psychology in Los Angeles.

Dr. Hein speaks both French and Spanish fluently, which is

probably a result of her love for people and her desire to communicate more fully with them.

She has appeared as the guest expert on *Oprah*, and on the radio show *Body Politics*. She lives in Santa Monica, California.